REPENT & BELIEVE

RELYING ON

GOD'S POWER

devoted
Discipleship Training for Small Groups

Repent & Believe: Relying on God's Power

Devoted: Discipleship Training for Small Groups

Copyright © 2018 by Clear Creek Community Church and Bruce Wesley

Editorial Team: Mandy Turner, Ryan Lehtinen, Jon Coffey

Published by Clear Creek Resources

A Ministry of Clear Creek Community Church

999 North FM 270

League City, Texas 77573

ISBN-13: 978-0-9979469-2-5

Unless otherwise indicated, all Scripture quotations are taken from:

The Holy Bible: English Standard Version, copyright © 2001 by Crossway Bibles, a division of Good News Publishers. Used by permission. All rights reserved.

All Scripture emphases have been added by the authors.

Printed in the United States of America

CONTENTS

INTRODUCTION

Can you name someone who discipled you?

When you look back on your early spiritual life, who taught you to believe the gospel of Jesus and submit yourself to him as the Lord of your life? Who taught you to worship and serve God? Who taught you to engage with God through the Bible and live as his representative in the world? We pose this question of discipleship frequently to groups of believers, and every crowd has a few hands go up. But most people cannot call the name of a person who discipled them. And since the axiom holds true that we tend to do with others what someone did with us, those who were not discipled by someone tend to not be personally involved in making disciples of others.

We want to change that! After all, Jesus spoke clearly about what he expects of his church in what's known as the Great Commission:

> Go therefore and make disciples of all nations, baptizing them in the name of the Father and of the Son and of the Holy Spirit, teaching them to observe all that I have commanded you. And behold, I am with you always, to the end of the age.
>
> Matthew 28:19-20

We want to train you to be a disciple. Additionally, we want you to engage in training someone else to be a disciple in the same way that you were trained. This pattern of disciples who make disciples is how the church can fulfill the Great Commission by multiplying disciples to the ends of the earth.

This material is designed for a small group to meet for thirty-nine weeks per year for two years. You will spend about two hours per week working through the material on your own, and then you will spend ninety minutes interacting with your group about what you are learning.

The *Devoted: Discipleship Training for Small Groups* series is grounded in the gospel of Jesus Christ. We explain how the gospel of Jesus Christ is instrumental in your spiritual growth through what we call The Spiritual Growth Grid. You will become extremely familiar with the grid, and you will become conversant in how it helps us grow as a disciple of Jesus.

As you participate in a small group, you will learn to be a disciple of Jesus Christ who:

Repent & Believe
- Relies on the power of God in your life
- Loves God with all your heart

Listen & Obey

- Hears God's voice
- Submits to God's will in all things

Love & Serve

- Lives interdependently with God's people
- Serves more than you are served

Goes & Multiply

- Shares the gospel in word and deed
- Articulates the gospel and its effects

Devoted: Discipleship Training for Small Groups includes eight studies of various lengths. The four topics each have two learning objectives, as shown above. The topic of this study is *Repent & Believe*, but there is more to be said about this topic than one study allows. So the first learning objective is for a disciple to learn to rely on God's power for life.

When you learn to repent and believe as a way of life, you will discover the operating system for spiritual growth. Let's get started.

Grace to you,
The Elders of Clear Creek Community Church

USING THE STUDY

Devoted is a two-year small group study series focused on training in the essentials of being a disciple who makes disciples. It is designed to help small groups grow deeper in the concepts of the Spiritual Growth Grid. This means, regardless of where you are on the spiritual journey, you play your part in the group each week when you:

Step 1: Memorize the Scripture

Throughout the study you will memorize key Bible passages specifically chosen for the topic. Practice reciting these each day. Try to fill in the blank spaces from memory as you prepare to recite the passages at your next small group meeting.

Step 2: Study the Scripture

The Bible passages are chosen because of the study's general theme. They are good Scriptures to know as either citizens, family, or missionaries. They don't necessarily relate directly to the day's teaching. This is a section where we want disciples to grow in the skill of observing and interpreting a text. The teaching that follows will deal with biblical application.

Step 3: Read the Teaching

Take your time to read through the day's teaching. The questions that follow are designed to help you better process the lesson in light of the Spiritual Growth Grid and apply the principles. Afterwards, take time to pray using the prompts provided.

Step 4: Do the Weekly Exercise

You will find a weekly exercise at the end of each week's Day 3 material. The exercises often employ different learning styles to practice the principles been taught. Be sure to not only do the exercise but the reflection section as well. The exercises are intended to help build your skill set as a disciple-making disciple.

Step 5: Ready Yourself for Group

The last section of each week's material concludes with the *Get Ready for Group* section. This allows you to summarize your key takeaways for the week in preparation for small group discussion. Please be sure to answer the final question concerning how the week's lessons help you better integrate the Spiritual Growth Grid. This will help your Navigator identify possible areas of further study in order to better live out one's gospel identity. Remember, the point is to be trained to be a disciple who makes disciples!

01

UNDERSTANDING REPENT & BELIEVE

SCRIPTURE MEMORY

Now after John was arrested, Jesus came into Galilee, proclaiming the gospel of God, and saying, "The time is fulfilled, and the kingdom of God is at hand; repent and believe in the gospel." *–Mark 1:14-15*

DAY
1

WHAT DOES IT MEAN TO REPENT AND BELIEVE?

Scripture Study

Mark 1:14-15

Now after John was arrested, Jesus came into Galilee, proclaiming the gospel of God, [15]and saying, "The time is fulfilled, and the kingdom of God is at hand; repent and believe in the gospel."

Observing the Text

Based on this passage, what is the message Jesus was continually proclaiming? Try to say it in your own words.

> The kingdom they had been waiting
> for was here & the way to access that
> kindom is to rearrange your life around the
> good news of God & trust Him for salvation.

Jesus announced a new opportunity. What's the opportunity? What makes it new?

> - To access the Kingdom
> - New: Needed Jesus to come first
>   - The time had to be fulfilled

Interpreting the Text

What do you think Jesus means by "the kingdom of God"? (See Matthew 6:10, Luke 17:21, Romans 14:17)

God's reign & rule

-where what God says goes

What do you think it means that "the Kingdom of God is at hand"?

Near

Here & Now

There is a pattern in the Bible where Jesus reveals something and then calls for a response. What response is Jesus calling for in this passage? What might that look like?

Repent & Believe

Turn & Trust

Teaching

When Jesus preached his message of good news to the world as seen in Mark 1:14-15, he said that the kingdom of God had become available. It was *at hand*. This meant, among other things, that Jesus made it possible for human beings to live their everyday lives under the reign of God. But just because Jesus made this possible doesn't mean it's automatic. A certain kind of response was required. Jesus called people to repent and believe, which was Jesus' way of saying that people must take a challenging journey from their current way of life to a brand new way of living as subjects of their new King, Jesus.

But how do we take this journey of repentance and belief? Is there a map? What must we know for the journey? This study will help followers learn to rely on God's power for life in his kingdom by learning to repent and believe as a way of life.

Repentance and belief go together. We can't do one without the other. Both are present tense, implying that disciples repent and believe continuously. So we can expect two aspects of repentance to keep showing up throughout our journey:

1. To repent is to change your mind about something.
Repentance comes from the Greek phrase *meta noia,* which literally means to change your mind. When we repent, we change what we believe and how we think; we change our mind about God. Maybe we did not believe in God, but now we do, or we thought God was disinterested, but now we believe he loves us. Perhaps we once thought Jesus was just another good man and religious leader, but now we believe Jesus is God who became a man to redeem us from sin and reconcile us to God.

Repentance also involves changing our mind about ourselves. We might have believed we were a good person who deserved God's goodness, but now we recognize ourselves as a sinner who deserves punishment. Maybe we once did not think we needed God, but now we realize that we need him desperately. We might have thought that our sin had forever disqualified us from God's family, but now we rejoice over our status as his forgiven child.

Discipleship is a process of changing our thoughts and beliefs to become like God's thoughts, whether the issue is money, sexuality, eternity, religion, friendship or any other topic. That's why the Bible is so important to our spiritual growth. We repent in light of what God says through his Word, and we change our mind about what we believe.

2. To repent is to reconsider our strategy for living.

Repentance turns a new way of thinking into a new way of living.

For example, most people are working through this material with a small group of people. Chances are, small group did not always fit into our strategy for living. Maybe we used to spend our time watching more TV, working late every night, or playing video games. But we rearranged our schedule to include small group because, now, we believe meeting with a small group is important for our spiritual life. That's one common way that followers of Jesus repent and believe.

So repentance is not just admitting a fault or feeling guilty for doing something wrong, which are common misunderstandings of repentance. Rather, it is completely reconsidering our strategy for living and rearranging our life around this new strategy where Jesus is king. New beliefs translate into habits of worshiping God, walking in community, serving people, and sharing our faith with others. Our new strategy for living might lead to personal changes too, like being less volatile in traffic, being honest in our work, and being diligent to resolve conflicts in ways that honor God.

The changes in our way of thinking and our strategy for living do not happen all of a sudden. It's a long journey. But when we repent and believe, we begin to experience a new way of life.

Questions for Reflection

Are there any ways in which you need to repent of beliefs about God's character or your own identity as his child that don't align with what God has said in his word?

- God wants to speak to me everyday
- I need to rearrange/reconsider my openness to hear His voice

What difference can it make when we refuse to believe falsehoods and begin to trust in what God has revealed in Scripture?

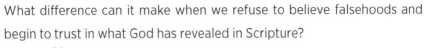

Changes Everything
- from "I think" to "this is God's revealed will"

Is God leading you to change your mind or reconsider your strategy for living about any issues in your life? If so, what is it?

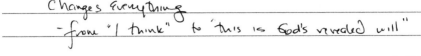

Right now, God has been revealing a need for renewed passion & for a real prayer life

In what ways are you finding it difficult to repent and believe?

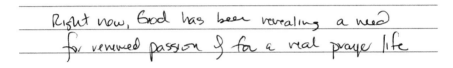

Making time

Prayer

Ask God to reveal any areas that you are unwilling to allow him to rule in your life. Thank him for the gift of repentance and belief when you crossed the line of faith, and ask him to help you to continue to respond to him with faith.

SCRIPTURE MEMORY

Now after John was arrested, Jesus came into Galilee, proclaiming the _Gospel_ of God, and saying, "The time is fulfilled, and the _Kingdom_ of God is at hand; repent and believe in the gospel." *–Mark 1:14-15*

THE OPERATING SYSTEM FOR SPIRITUAL GROWTH

Scripture Study

Acts 26:12-20

"In this connection I journeyed to Damascus with the authority and commission of the chief priests. ¹³ At midday, O king, I saw on the way a light from heaven, brighter than the sun, that shone around me and those who journeyed with me. ¹⁴ And when we had all fallen to the ground, I heard a voice saying to me in the Hebrew language] 'Saul, Saul, why are you persecuting me? It is hard for you to kick against the goads.' ¹⁵ And I said, 'Who are you, Lord?' And the Lord said, 'I am Jesus whom you are persecuting. ¹⁶ But rise and stand upon your feet, for I have appeared to you for this purpose, to appoint you as a servant and witness to the things in which you have seen me and to those in which I will appear to you, ¹⁷ delivering you from your people and from the Gentiles—to whom I am sending you ¹⁸ to open their eyes, so that they may turn from darkness to light and from the power of Satan to God, that they may receive forgiveness of sins and a place among those who are sanctified by faith in me.'

[19] *"Therefore, O King Agrippa, I was not disobedient to the heavenly vision,* [20] *but declared first to those in Damascus, then in Jerusalem and through-out all the region of Judea, and also to the Gentiles, that they should repent and turn to God, performing deeds in keeping with their repentance."*

Observing the text

Where did Paul's repentance begin?

Road to Damascus

How does Paul's testimony illustrate repentance?

Was going to persecute in one direction & b/c of encounter w/ Jesus reconsidered & then chose to follow Him instead

Interpreting the text

In Paul's words to King Agrippa, how does Paul expect to recognize others' repentance?

performing deeds of repentance

What are some "deeds in keeping with repentance" that we would hope to see in one another?

honesty   kindness
humility   love
generosity   sincerity

Teaching

Imagine you have a program on your computer that captures and stores your thoughts. Furthermore, it enables you to move words or whole paragraphs with a few simple keystrokes. It even allows you to store your thoughts for retrieval later. That's amazing! Now you might be one of those people who never knew what life was like without a computer and a word-processing program. Some of us did most of our academic work on typewriters. If you don't know what that is, look it up on your computer.

Word-processing programs on the computer have changed the way we work. As helpful as it may be, a word-processing program is not enough by itself.

All of the amazing programs on your computer are worthless without something that probably most of us don't think about much. In order to access the program, your computer uses something called an operating system. The operating system does not do the work that the word-processing program can do, but it allows you to get to the program. Tech-savvy people explain it this way.

> An operating system is the most important software that runs on a computer. It manages the computer's memory and processes, as well as all of its software and hardware. It also allows you to communicate with the computer without knowing how to speak the computer's language. Without an operating system, a computer is useless.[1]

Life with God changes the way we live far more than any word processor.

---

1 http://www.gcflearnfree.org/computerbasics/understanding-operating-systems

As a disciple, we can receive God's direction for life, live as a member of God's family, and impact eternity as part of God's mission in the world. But there is an "operating system" that allows us to connect with God's amazing gifts as we grow spiritually. That operating system is our repentance and belief in the gospel.

On October 31, 1517, a monk named Martin Luther nailed his list of ninety-five statements to the door of a church in Wittenburg. He wanted to debate a wayward practice of the church at that time called "indulgences." His first statement read, "When our Lord and Master Jesus Christ said 'Repent,' he intended that the entire life of believers should be repentance."

All of the Christian life is repentance. Turning from sin and trusting in the good news that Jesus saves sinners is the daily practice of a disciple.

Repentance is the operating system required to connect us with the amazing life God makes possible. That's why our spiritual growth grid begins with *Repent & Believe*.

REPENT & BELIEVE			
WHO GOD IS (Identity)	**WHAT GOD DID** (Activity)	**WHO WE ARE** (Identity)	**WHAT WE DO** (Activity)
KING	CALLED	CITIZENS	LISTEN & OBEY
FATHER	ADOPTED	FAMILY	LOVE & SERVE
SAVIOR	SENT	MISSIONARIES	GO & MULTIPLY

The path to knowing God as King, Father, and Savior requires that we repent and believe. Before we can live a life as citizens in God's kingdom, children in God's family, and missionaries sent by God, we must repent and believe. In order to listen and obey, love and serve, or go and multiply, we must first repent and believe. It's the operating system to access God's plan for our lives.

Repentance and belief aren't just one-time responses when we first understand the gospel. Rather, every day for the rest of our lives we repent and believe as a regular practice of our lives.

Questions for Reflection

Is a regular pattern of repentance and belief characterizing your life right now? What do we tend to base our spiritual life on when we're avoiding repentance? How is this evident to your family, spouse, or small group?

- I think so — after I pray similar prayers as a baseline / foundation
- When I'm not - tend to base spiritual life on performance

What will be the results if Christians neglect to participate in continual repentance and belief? How can this affect their spiritual growth?

Over-Confidence (Pride)
    or   Despair
- Stunts spiritual growth on either end

How have you experienced these negative outcomes when repentance and belief were not priorities?

I can tend to be too self-dependent which leads to dry spiritual seasons

Prayer

Pray that Christ would turn your heart to base your relationship with him on continually responding to him with faith and repentance. Thank him for making that relationship possible through his death on the cross.

SCRIPTURE MEMORY

Now after John was arrested, Jesus came into Galilee, _proclaiming_ the gospel of God, and saying, "The _time_ is fulfilled, and the _kingdom_ of God is at hand; repent and believe in the gospel." –*Mark 1:14-15*

A DISCIPLE RELIES ON GOD'S POWER

Scripture Study

Acts 26:12-20

"In this connection I journeyed to Damascus with the authority and commission of the chief priests. [13] At midday, O king, I saw on the way a light from heaven, brighter than the sun, that shone around me and those who journeyed with me. [14] And when we had all fallen to the ground, I heard a voice saying to me in the Hebrew language] 'Saul, Saul, why are you persecuting me? It is hard for you to kick against the goads.' [15] And I said, 'Who are you, Lord?' And the Lord said, 'I am Jesus whom you are persecuting. [16] But rise and stand upon your feet, for I have appeared to you for this purpose, to appoint you as a servant and witness to the things in which you have seen me and to those in which I will appear to you, [17] delivering you from your people and from the Gentiles — to whom I am sending you [18] to open their eyes, so that they may turn from darkness to light and from the power of Satan to God, that they may receive forgiveness of sins and a place among those who are sanctified by faith in me.'

[19] "Therefore, O King Agrippa, I was not disobedient to the heavenly vision,

²⁰ but declared first to those in Damascus, then in Jerusalem and through-out all the region of Judea, and also to the Gentiles, that they should repent and turn to God, performing deeds in keeping with their repentance."

Observing the Text

What two things does Paul say people must do to repent?

Turn to God

Live it out

What words or phrases in this story can help us understand the nature of repentance?

turn to God

turn from darkness to light

from Satan to God

Interpreting the Text

How does Paul's calling from God speak to repentance?

God initiates

In what ways do you think Paul's encounter with Jesus empowered him for ministry?

It wasn't his own doing

- confident in God's work, not his own

Teaching

This *Devoted* study series begins with a focus on the call of all disciples to repent and believe. It is further titled *Relying on God's Power*. What does relying on God's power have to do with repentance and belief?

Let's ask the question another way. Let's say you are struggling with a sin in your life, as we all do. Let's imagine that you struggle with becoming angry and hurting the people you love with harsh words and hurtful actions. You don't want to keep behaving this way. You want to change. Where do you expect to get the power to change?

You might make promises to yourself that you are serious this time, and you are determined to change. You might go to a bookstore to see if there is a book that can help. You might ask for help from a friend who seems to be at peace all the time. You might make an appointment with a psychologist who can help you get to the root of your anger. All of these options might help, but as disciples we cannot place our faith in any of these for the power to change. Instead, we must repent, believing that Jesus is the only one who can bring about real transformation.

We can only experience true change with God's power when we restructure our lives around two essentials — one is God's part, and the other is ours. First, to rely on God's power, we must be *filled with the Holy Spirit*. That's God's part; only he can fill us. Second, to rely on God's power, we must *practice spiritual disciplines*, or what has been known in church history as a Rule of Life. That's our part. The remainder of this study will lead you to reconsider your strategy for living so that you rely on God's power by being filled with the Holy Spirit and practicing spiritual disciplines.

Questions for Reflection

What power sources have you relied upon in your life when you have trials, problems, or a desire to change? In what ways have they been effective? In what ways have they failed you?

Grit/Hard Work ⟶ lead to exhaustion
Friends ⟶ not enough
God/Wisdom ⟶ humble - confidence

How is fear or uncertainty inhibiting your belief that God is powerful enough to create change in your life?

What hinders or distracts you from continually turning away from unbelief and turning to God in faith?

Time

Prayer

Praise God for his infinite power to change our lives through the work of the Spirit. Ask him to open your eyes to ways you have tried to change without his power.

WEEKLY
EXERCISE

POWER FAILURE

Make a list of three areas in your life where you have experienced a personal failure to rely on the right power. Be prepared to share some of these areas of power failure with your small group.

1. SELF-RELIANCE

2. ANGER / IRRITABILITY w/ KIDS

3. Selfishness

....

Don't despair. With these areas of personal power failure in mind, read these passages out loud and meditate on the truth in them regarding your identity and God's character.

> *No temptation has overtaken you that is not common to man. God is faithful, and he will not let you be tempted beyond your ability, but with the temptation he will also provide the way of escape, that you may be able to endure it. Therefore, my beloved, flee from idolatry.*
> 1 Corinthians 10:13-14

> *There is therefore now no condemnation for those who are in Christ Jesus. For the law of the Spirit of life has set you free in Christ Jesus from the law of sin and death. For God has done what the law, weakened by the flesh, could not do. By sending his own Son in the likeness of sinful flesh and for sin, he condemned sin in the flesh, in order that the righteous require-*

ment of the law might be fulfilled in us, who walk not according to the flesh but according to the Spirit.

Romans 8:1-4

Keep your life free from love of money, and be content with what you have, for he has said, "I will never leave you nor forsake you." So we can confidently say, "The Lord is my helper; I will not fear; what can man do to me?"

Hebrews 13:5-6

What then shall we say to these things? If God is for us, who can be against us? He who did not spare his own Son but gave him up for us all, how will he not also with him graciously give us all things? Who shall bring any charge against God's elect? It is God who justifies. Who is to condemn? Christ Jesus is the one who died—more than that, who was raised—who is at the right hand of God, who indeed is interceding for us. Who shall separate us from the love of Christ? Shall tribulation, or distress, or persecution, or famine, or nakedness, or danger, or sword? As it is written, "For your sake we are being killed all the day long; we are regarded as sheep to be slaughtered." No, in all these things we are more than conquerors through him who loved us. For I am sure that neither death nor life, nor angels nor rulers, nor things present nor things to come, nor powers, nor height nor depth, nor anything else in all creation, will be able to separate us from the love of God in Christ Jesus our Lord.

Romans 8:31-39

Get Ready for Group

Write your memorized scripture.

Now after John was arrested, Jesus came into Galilee proclaiming The gospel of God and saying, "The time is fulfilled & Kingdom of God is at hand, repent & believe in The gospel."

— Mark 1:14-15

What observations and interpretations of scripture were most meaningful to you?

Acts 26

Repentance — turn to God, live in repentance
from dark to light
from Satan to God

Summarize your key takeaway(s) for this week.

Whole life is repentance
Repentance & Belief
gives power
for life transformation

What will you tell the group about the results of your exercise this week?

Share areas of
Power failure

How has this week helped you better understand and apply the Spiritual Growth Grid?

R&B — foundation

REPENT & BELIEVE			
WHO GOD IS	**WHAT GOD DID**	**WHO WE ARE**	**WHAT WE DO**
KING	CALLED	CITIZENS	LISTEN & OBEY
FATHER	ADOPTED	FAMILY	LOVE & SERVE
SAVIOR	SENT	MISSIONARIES	GO & MULTIPLY

02

HOW OBEDIENCE WORKS

SCRIPTURE MEMORY

Now after John was arrested, Jesus came into Galilee, proclaiming the gospel of God, and saying, "The time is fulfilled, and the kingdom of God is at hand; repent and believe in the gospel." *–Mark 1:14-15*

WHERE OBEDIENCE BEGINS

Scripture Study

Galatians 4:1-9

I mean that the heir, as long as he is a child, is no different from a slave, though he is the owner of everything, ² but he is under guardians and managers until the date set by his father. ³ In the same way we also, when we were children, were enslaved to the elementary principles of the world. ⁴ But when the fullness of time had come, God sent forth his Son, born of woman, born under the law, ⁵ to redeem those who were under the law, so that we might receive adoption as sons. ⁶ And because you are sons, God has sent the Spirit of his Son into our hearts, crying, "Abba! Father!" ⁷ So you are no longer a slave, but a son, and if a son, then an heir through God.

⁸ Formerly, when you did not know God, you were enslaved to those that by nature are not gods. ⁹ But now that you have come to know God, or rather to be known by God, how can you turn back again to the weak and worthless elementary principles of the world, whose slaves you want to be once more?

Observing the Text

What analogy does Paul use in this passage to describe the Christian experience?

Adoption
from Slave to Son

In verse 9, what action does Paul consider ridiculous for one who is now an heir?

Turning back to slavery (old ways of living)

Interpreting the Text

According to this passage, in what ways did your identity change when you crossed the line of faith? How does this change occur?

Become a Son — inheriting all that the father has
— Adoption — by God's grace

What does it look like when an heir begins to revert to the former life of slavery? In what ways is that a failure of belief, rather than just a behavioral failure?

Turning back
forget whose you are & who you are

Teaching

Last week, we learned that to repent is to "change your mind about something" and to "reconsider your strategy for living." Repentance then becomes our lifestyle because trusting in Jesus as our King leads to a whole new way of thinking and a different strategy for living. We learned that repentance works like a spiritual operating system, enabling us to rely on God's power instead of our own. But in order for us to be empowered by God's strength, we must (1) be filled with the Holy Spirit and (2) practice a Rule of Life. Being filled with the Spirit is God's part. Practicing a Rule of Life is our part.

> And Jesus came and said to them, "All authority in heaven and on earth has been given to me. Go therefore and make disciples of all nations, baptizing them in the name of the Father and of the Son and of the Holy Spirit, teaching them to observe all that I have commanded you. And behold, I am with you always, to the end of the age."
>
> Matthew 28:18-20

The NIV translates verse 20 as *teaching them to obey all that I commanded you*. In order to understand Jesus' command for his disciples to obey him, we must understand the general concept in the Bible that God desires to move people from one realm into another. God speaks of these two realms in numerous ways. The chart below depicts some of the ways the Bible speaks of these two realms.

Sinful Realm moving *from* this realm	→	Gospel Realm *into* this realm
The Fallen Earth		The New Heaven and New Earth
The Reign of Sin		The Kingdom of God
Slaves to Sin		Sons of God
The life of Adam		The life of Christ
Not a people		The people of God
The Old		The New

In the beginning and the ending of the Bible, God emphasizes the two realms. In Genesis 1-3, God's realm is a beautiful garden where Adam and Eve walk with him in perfect relationship. But when they sin, they are removed from the realm of God's garden. They experience the realm of sin, where there is guilt, shame, and death. They experience life in a realm where God's will is not always done. Then, at the end of the Bible in Revelation 22, God's realm is described as a city and a garden, and God is dwelling again with his people. The grand story of God's redeeming work culminates with God making all things new. God's people live forever in God's kingdom where he shall reign forever and ever. The paradise lost is now regained.

But between Genesis 1-3 and Revelation 22, the Bible shows how people experience both realms at the same time. We describe this experience by saying the kingdom of God is "already/not yet." This is earth, not heaven.

Already, God has moved us into his realm through the gospel. We have a new identity as God's children. Once, we were not his people; now we are the people of God. We were slaves to sin, but now we are the heirs of God. We were citizens of the kingdoms of this world, but now we are citizens in the kingdom of God. We have a foretaste of life in the Spirit (Ephesians 1:13). We are already forgiven and given amazing promises of an eternal kind of life.

But we have not yet left all of the effects of the realm of sin. We have not yet learned to trust God completely as king over us. We have not yet been delivered from the power and presence of sin. We have not yet experienced all that God promises in salvation. We fall down. We disobey. We make mistakes.

Obedience comes into play between the *already* and the *not yet*. Through obedience to God and his commands, we are learning to live in the new realm for which God saved us. All of God's commands are for our good and his glory! Through God's Law (rooted in the Ten Commandments) and Jesus' words and other commands in the scriptures, God sanctifies us by empowering us to live out the work he has already done in our lives. Said another way, *in obedience, we learn to act like the person God has already made us to become.* We are growing in our ability to live in the new realm.

Therefore, obedience begins with a new identity. The realm you are in should determine the way that you will live.

Greg Poore, the Associate Pastor at CCCC, told us once about a man who spent 80 days traversing Antarctica. He had to make unbelievable concessions to that drastic environment: multiple layers of gloves and socks, wind and water-proof outer layers, boots with insulated soles. He would even eat sticks of raw butter in order to take in the 5000-9000 calories needed to sustain him on each day of the trek. What it would be like to transfer that guy out of the arctic to a tropical region? Just imagine strolling the beach on Oahu next to a snowshoeing, parka-wearing explorer munching on a stick of butter! Any bystander would think he was crazy. Why? Because no one's behavior in Hawaii should be the same as how they lived in Antarctica. As Greg said, *"How you live should fit where you live."*

Obedience begins with identity. That's why the Spiritual Growth Grid emphasizes identity before activity. We must always begin with who we are. If we are not clear on our identity, obedience will be even more elusive. Instead, we will act like we are still in the old realm, snowshoeing on tropical beaches.

Remember Paul's words: *"If anyone is in Christ, he is a new creation"* (2 Corinthians 5:17). As soon as we come to faith in Jesus, we are citizens who have been called into his kingdom, we are children of God adopted into his family, and we are missionaries sent on his mission. We are in the process of learning to live in our new identity. We are learning to arrange our lives in the way that he wants us to arrange our lives. We are learning to believe what a citizen of his realm believes.

Questions for Reflection

What are the difficulties inherent in the Christian's already/not yet experience? In what ways have you felt the tensions of existing between two realms?

- Knowing what I "should do" versus feeling a pull towards what I "want to do".
- Living in a world that doesn't submit to God, isn't interested in his reign/rule

What does it look like when a believer isn't living in God's realm? In other words, what might your parka and boots be that you are wearing on the beach?

- Characterized by sin & selfishness
- Looks a lot more like the world

Write the words you imagine God might say to you to help you embrace your new identity.

You are my Son.
Act like it.

Prayer

Thank God for adopting you into his family and bringing you into the realm of his Son. Ask him reveal any ways in which you're returning to the realm of slavery to sin, praying for his power to daily live in his kingdom.

SCRIPTURE MEMORY

Now after John was arrested, Jesus came into GALILEE, proclaiming the Gospel of God, and saying, "The time is fulfilled, and the kingdom of God is at HAND; repent and believe in the gospel." *–Mark 1:14-15*

BELIEF BEFORE BEHAVIOR

Scripture Study

Genesis 3:1-13

Now the serpent was more crafty than any other beast of the field that the LORD God had made.

He said to the woman, "Did God actually say, 'You shall not eat of any tree in the garden'?" ² And the woman said to the serpent, "We may eat of the fruit of the trees in the garden, ³ but God said, 'You shall not eat of the fruit of the tree that is in the midst of the garden, neither shall you touch it, lest you die.'" ⁴ But the serpent said to the woman, "You will not surely die. ⁵ For God knows that when you eat of it your eyes will be opened, and you will be like God, knowing good and evil." ⁶ So when the woman saw that the tree was good for food, and that it was a delight to the eyes, and that the tree was to be desired to make one wise, she took of its fruit and ate, and she also gave some to her husband who was with her, and he ate. ⁷ Then the eyes of both were opened, and they knew that they were naked. And they sewed fig leaves together and made themselves loincloths.

8 And they heard the sound of the LORD God walking in the garden in the cool of the day, and the man and his wife hid themselves from the presence of the LORD God among the trees of the garden. 9 But the LORD God called to the man and said to him, "Where are you?" 10 And he said, "I heard the sound of you in the garden, and I was afraid, because I was naked, and I hid myself." 11 He said, "Who told you that you were naked? Have you eaten of the tree of which I commanded you not to eat?" 12 The man said, "The woman whom you gave to be with me, she gave me fruit of the tree, and I ate." 13 Then the LORD God said to the woman, "What is this that you have done?" The woman said, "The serpent deceived me, and I ate."

Observing the Text

What lies did Satan tell Eve about the fruit? How did she respond to his words?

"Did God actually say"

"Surely you won't die"

"You'll be like God, knowing good devil."

What was the result of their failure to obey God's commands?

Separation from God
& hiding & blaming

Interpreting the Text

What did Eve believe about the forbidden fruit? How does her behavior reveal her beliefs about who God is and what he wants for them?

It would make her like God
- She wanted more then what God offered
wanted to be there
- didn't trust God's provision for her
& who He said she was

How does their failure to believe God impact their relationship with him?

Causes fear, distance, separation

Teaching

Sometimes people get stuck in destructive patterns of disobedience. It's common to hear from people whose anger has killed their marriage, whose inability to manage money has left them in financial bondage, or whose poor health habits have left them feeling shame and lacking energy. They might say, "I want to change the way I act, but I keep doing the same old things I was doing before. I make commitments, but I don't keep them." Why?

One of the keys to understanding how we can change and begin to obey God has to do with beliefs.

> *Do not be conformed to this world, but be transformed by the renewal of your mind, that by testing you may discern what is the will of God, what is good and acceptable and perfect.*
>
> Romans 12:2

Obedience requires a change in our beliefs. When our thinking changes, our lives change as a result. *Belief comes before behavior.* Our beliefs are the software of the soul, determining the applications and functions of our lives. The beliefs we hold influence our feelings which then dictate our behavior.

Beliefs ⟶ Feelings ⟶ Behaviors

The book *Sleeping with Bread* tells a story about orphan children during World War II who had great difficulty sleeping after being rescued and placed in refugee camps. Eventually their caregivers discovered that giving the children a piece of bread to hold would enable them to sleep through the night. The children were afraid to sleep because they had so much uncertainty about having enough to eat the next day. But when their belief changed about their food, it then changed how they slept. Their beliefs determined their feelings. And their feelings determined their behavior.

Behaviors are easier to see than beliefs. Each of us bears the fruit of good and life-giving beliefs and the scars of destructive and painful beliefs. We behave the way we do because of what we believe.

The Bible clearly demonstrates that we are capable of changing what we believe. None of our beliefs are pre-installed as the software of our soul. We are learning new beliefs and changing all the time. That's why the apostle Paul could instruct us to not be conformed to the belief systems of this world, but instead to be changed by reshaping our beliefs, or renewing our minds.

Paul knew that in order to change the world, we have to change the belief systems of the world. And in order to change ourselves, we have to change our belief system as well.

> *For the weapons of our warfare are not of the flesh but have divine power to destroy strongholds. We destroy arguments and every lofty opinion raised against the knowledge of God, and take every thought captive to obey Christ, being ready to punish every disobedience, when your obedience is complete.*
>
> 2 Corinthians 10:4-6

In this passage, Paul shows that we are entrenched in a battle of convictions. False beliefs are perpetuated by spiritual forces of evil. This spiritual battle is on the field of arguments, where false ideas strain against the knowledge of God — who God truly is and what he is like. Followers of Christ are called to learn the discipline of taking every thought captive. Some thoughts are errant thoughts. Haven't you had a wild and atrocious thought track through your head? That's part of living in the "not yet" of this present world. In order to learn obedience, we take those thoughts captive: we change what we think about and what we believe.

> Progress is impossible without change, and those who cannot change their minds cannot change anything.
>
> —George Bernard Shaw

Beliefs come from what we are told. Beliefs are the voices inside your head. In order to change our beliefs, we need to be told something new. We need to hear a new voice — a voice of truth. That's why God gave us the gospel and the entirety of scripture. He's speaking truth to us.

What have you wanted to change about your behavior? In what area have you desired to obey, but you find yourself stuck? Remember: beliefs *before* behavior. You must change your beliefs to change your behavior from sin to obedience.

Once you pinpoint a behavior you want to change, consider what false beliefs have driven that behavior. What thoughts do you need to reject? What truth about God, his Word, others, or yourself do you need to believe?

Don't rush through this. Don't move on because you understand the concept. This is the hard work of repentance. It's where real spiritual formation happens. We identify and reject our false beliefs. We rehearse and embrace the truth. When beliefs take root, so will obedience.

Questions for Reflection

How would you explain the close connection between our actions and the voices we believe?

How we live, act, behave is always an overflow of what we believe / think about ourselves & God

What have you wanted to change about your behavior? In what area have you desired to obey, but you find yourself stuck?

Anger / Irritability

What false beliefs have driven that behavior?

That life should go my, kids should obey me & I'd get what I want how I want it

What truth about God, his Word, others, or yourself do you need to believe?

Life is about God & the Kingdom not me & mine

Prayer

Ask God to help you take every thought captive that battles against the truth, praying that he would display his beauty and goodness as more desirable than any forbidden fruit. Thank him for the gift of Scripture, where he is shown to be the source of all truth.

SCRIPTURE MEMORY

Now after John was arrested, _Jesus_

came into Galilee, proclaiming the

Gospel of God, and saying, "The

time is fulfilled, and the _Kingdom_ of

God is at hand; repent and believe

in the gospel." *—Mark 1:14-15*

A RADICAL STEP

Scripture Study

Matthew 5:27-30

You have heard that it was said, "You shall not commit adultery." [28] *But I say to you that everyone who looks at a woman with lustful intent has already committed adultery with her in his heart.* [29] *If your right eye causes you to sin, tear it out and throw it away. For it is better that you lose one of your members than that your whole body be thrown into hell.* [30] *And if your right hand causes you to sin, cut it off and throw it away. For it is better that you lose one of your members than that your whole body go into hell.*

Observing the Text

Jesus is quoting from the Ten Commandments in verse 27. In what way does he expand the extent of the original command?

That obedience is about more than just "action"; It's about the heart

What does Jesus say should be our response to the sins we commit?

Take Drastic Measures to cut out sin

Interpreting the Text

Do you think we should read Jesus' words here as a literal command? Why or why not?

No, it's hyperbole
1) God doesn't ever condone self-harm or self-flagellation
2) People/Jesus disciples would be walking around w/ one eye & arm all the time

What do Jesus' words show us about whether or not he takes sin seriously?

He takes it very seriously

Teaching

Jesus calls for radical steps toward change. We can not stay the same and change at the same time.

Matthew 5-7, known as the Sermon on the Mount, is Jesus' description of life in his kingdom. The key verse is Matthew 5:20.

> *For I tell you, unless your righteousness exceeds that of the scribes and Pharisees, you will never enter the kingdom of heaven.*

Jesus is preaching a new way of relating to God that goes beyond the legalistic religion where people keep score about how many good or bad things they do. God's righteousness is more than merely keeping the letter of the law; it embraces the spirit of the law. That's why Jesus often uses the formula, "You have heard it said...but I say to you," in his teaching. The

Higher or lower bar?

Greg's sermon yesterday ("/3)

first part of the formula states the letter of the law. The part that Jesus adds calls us to obey the spirit of the law.

In Matthew 5:27-30, Jesus applies this formula to the issue of adultery. His call goes beyond the refusal to have intercourse with someone other than your spouse. He addresses the spirit of the original command so that obedience comes from the heart, not just obligation.

Jesus knows that the heart is the water table of one's life. If you poison the heart, you poison everything. He doesn't want lust to poison everything in a person's life. So, Jesus suggests a radical step.

What does Jesus say a man is to do if he lusts for a woman? Dig out your eyeball. Tear it loose from the socket! Break all the connective nerves and tissue, and drop that eyeball in the garbage can with the coffee grounds and banana peels. Ouch! That's horrible. But Jesus isn't finished. If you've been longing to use that right hand to touch a woman who is not your wife, sharpen up a meat cleaver and chop it off. Then toss it in the garbage too.

You might think, "Whoa! That's crazy!" And you would be right. Jesus isn't speaking literally. He's exaggerating to make his point. (So, don't blind or dismember yourself.) We don't see any of Jesus' followers in the Bible plucking out their eyes or cutting off their hands, even though one or two of them might have lusted for someone.

While Jesus is not speaking literally, he is speaking seriously. It really would be better to be blind and dismembered than to be thrown into hell. If we understood what it's like to be in hell, we might do something crazy to keep from going there, even if it blinded us in one eye.

Listen. Hands are good. Eyes are good. Obedience from the heart is even better.

Radical steps are necessary for obedience, because a lack of intentionality will never lead us toward godliness and kingdom living. Rather, we will drift into a life of sin where we leave God out and do things our way. A glance turns into a look, which turns into a fantasy, which turns into a plan, which turns into a conversation which turns into more and more. Jesus says we should take a radical step for obedience before we start down the road toward more and more.

If a man struggles with lust, he might need to get rid of cable. He may need to put accountability software on his computer. He might just need to get rid of internet at home! Some might say, "What? How would I explain that?" You might think that sounds radical, but it's not as radical as tearing out your eye!

What Jesus is talking about here isn't limited to lust. Money is an idol in our culture, and many Christians fail to honor God with their money. They either don't give God the first ten percent, or if they do, they may not surrender their spending decisions to God. Some use every penny they have in pursuit of their own pleasure, or they are so deep in debt from living this way for years that they feel like they can't obey now. But radical change is possible. There are people who were so ready to obey God regarding money that they sold their house to get out of debt. They sold their brand new car and bought an older car, so that they no longer had a car payment. They developed a budget. They gave to God first. Does any of that sound crazy? It's not as crazy as cutting off your own hand.

You can't stay the same and change at the same time. You can't leave things the way they are and obey in ways that are different.

In what way do you need to obey God? Take a moment. Consider the area of your life where you most want to turn from sin and obey God's commands instead. Now, what would be the radical steps that would protect you against sin or make room for you to have the will to obey? Don't rush through this. Don't pluck out your eye or cut off your hand, but a radical step might be just what you need. You will want to begin with your beliefs and then move to your behavior.

Questions for Reflection

In what way do you need to obey God?

Pray & Hear from God everyday

In what ways are you minimizing the significance of your sin? When we fail to recognize the seriousness of our sin, how are our relationships and witness to others impacted?

- Compare to others rather than God's standard
- when I'm not right spiritually — not as good of a husband, father, friend, Missionary

What beliefs are at the root of your minimization of that sin? What radical steps of obedience do you need to take today in order to take righteousness seriously?

Go to bed early, Get enough sleep
Prioritize Hearing from God & working out
Running
Sleeping In

What radical steps of obedience do you need to take today in order to take righteousness seriously?

Pray now
Sleep Well tonight - get week started right

Prayer

Spend time examining your life for areas where you haven't treated sin with the seriousness that it deserves, and pray for eyes that see sin's destructiveness in the way that Jesus does. Ask God to give you the strength to take radical steps of obedience.

WEEKLY EXERCISE

PREPARING FOR OBEDIENCE

This exercise will help you think through a pathway to obedience by applying the lessons from this week. Review the example to see how each question relates to obedience. Then, work through the questions regarding an area of your life where you want to grow in obedience.

....

EXAMPLE

Identify a sin or an area of disobedience in your life.

> *"I disobey God with money"*

OLD REALM

Describe what disobedience looks like in this area of your life.

> *"Not giving faithfully, too much debt, not seeking God's guidance regarding spending"*

What false beliefs are behind the disobedience?

> *"I believe the more my family has, the happier they will be. I believe that if I give God control of my money, I will not have enough. "*

How do those false beliefs make you feel?

> *"I feel cheated if my family doesn't have what others have. The thought of following Jesus' teachings regarding money causes me to feel fear about the future."*

NEW REALM

Describe what obedience would look like in this area of your life?

> *"Living with budgeted priorities for giving, saving, and spending."*
> *"Getting out of debt so that I have financial margin."*

What beliefs must you embrace in order to obey? What Bible passages reinforce your new beliefs?

"God is my provider. He is a good Father who takes care of his children."

"God wants me to give to him first."

"God wants me to learn to trust him with my future and not worry about tomorrow."

Matthew 6:19-21, Matthew 6:25-34, 1 Timothy 6:6-10, 2 Corinthians 9:6-11

How do those beliefs make you feel?

"Dependent. A little afraid."

What is your plan for changing your behavior?

"I will rearrange my financial obligations."

"I will work with my spouse to develop a budget that reflects my trust in God. "

"I will pray about my finances and remind myself of the passages in the Bible that reinforce my beliefs."

....

Now you try. The exercise is not about having the right answers. It's about rehearsing how obedience works as we learn to repent and believe.

Identify a sin or an area of disobedience in your life

Lack of intentional prayer time

OLD REALM

Describe what disobedience looks like in this area of your life.

Knowing God wants me to pray & choosing my way, my priorities ove this

What false beliefs are behind the disobedience?

"I can do it on my own"
"I'm too busy."

How do those false beliefs make you feel?

I feel weak when I admit fault or dependence.

Describe what obedience would look like in this area of your life?

Carving out additional time to pray, not just read scripture w/ devotional

What beliefs must you embrace in order to obey? What Bible passages reinforce your new beliefs?

God wants to speak to me & wants me to speak with Him throughout the day, not just in segmented times I "set aside"
1 Thess 5:17 - Pray w/o ceasing
Col 4:2 - Continue steadfastly in prayer, being watchful in it w/ thanksgiving

How do those beliefs make you feel?

God loves me more than I think sometimes

What is your plan for changing your behavior?

Prioritizing prayer in the morning
Setting alarms on my phone:
10:45

2:00

4:30
Pray w/ Bethany at night
before TV

Get Ready for Group

Write your memorized scripture.

Mark 1:14-15

Now after John was arrested Jesus came into Galilee proclaiming the Gospel of God & saying, "The time is fulfilled? The Kingdom of God is at hand, repent & believe in the Gospel."

What observations and interpretations of scripture were most meaningful to you?

Matt 5 — Spirit of the law
- not a lower bar but a higher one
- God takes sin seriously & my desire to obey Him comes from my identity in Christ

Summarize your key takeaway(s) for this week.

You cannot stay the same & change at the same time.
Insanity — doing the same thing. expect diff results

Already — Not Yet
- where obedience lives
- learn to act like the person God has made us to be

What will you tell the group about the results of your exercise this week?

Trouble identifying a habitual sin tendency
- I sin & am selfish
- I can lust or be prideful but it's not a consistent lifestyle

How has this week helped you better understand and apply the Spiritual Growth Grid?

WHO WE ARE (IDENTITY)
Is a work in progress
- between The already & not yet

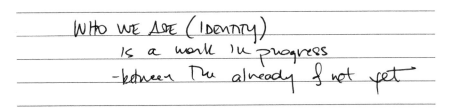

03

GOD'S PART AND OUR PART

SCRIPTURE MEMORY

Now after John was arrested, Jesus came into Galilee, proclaiming the gospel of God, and saying, "The time is fulfilled, and the kingdom of God is at hand; repent and believe in the gospel." *–Mark 1:14-15*

GOD'S PART

Scripture Study

John 15:1-8

I am the true vine, and my Father is the vinedresser. ² Every branch in me that does not bear fruit he takes away, and every branch that does bear fruit he prunes, that it may bear more fruit. ³ Already you are clean because of the word that I have spoken to you. ⁴ Abide in me, and I in you. As the branch cannot bear fruit by itself, unless it abides in the vine, neither can you, unless you abide in me. ⁵ I am the vine; you are the branches. Whoever abides in me and I in him, he it is that bears much fruit, for apart from me you can do nothing. ⁶ If anyone does not abide in me he is thrown away like a branch and withers; and the branches are gathered, thrown into the fire, and burned. ⁷ If you abide in me, and my words abide in you, ask whatever you wish, and it will be done for you. ⁸ By this my Father is glorified, that you bear much fruit and so prove to be my disciples.

Observing the Text

Write out the analogy that Jesus uses in your own words, as though you were explaining it to a ten-year-old.

_____

_____

What does the passage say God does so that those connected to him will bear fruit?

_____

_____

_____

Interpreting the Text

What does it mean to "bear much fruit"? (See also Galatians 5:22-23)

_____

_____

_____

What does the vine analogy illustrate about God's part in our spiritual formation?

_____

_____

_____

What does it mean to be "cut off" or "pruned"? Is there a difference?

_____

_____

_____

Teaching

Understanding our identity in Christ will dramatically impact how we behave. Embracing our new identity as citizens in God's kingdom, children in God's family, and missionaries on God's mission is a first step toward obedience. But our spiritual growth isn't only about what we do.

Spiritual life requires the work and power of God the Holy Spirit. This is what Jesus meant in John 15:5 when he said, *"Apart from me you can do nothing."* If you cut branches from a vine and let them sit in a pile for a few days, it becomes obvious that they are dead. The life of the vine was required for the branches to remain alive and bear fruit. In the same way, we are completely dependent upon God to produce spiritual life and spiritual fruit in us. If we are cut off from God, we die. If we grow, it's because God grew us. If we change, it's because God changed us.

As you read the following passages, look for what God does for our growth:

And I will ask the Father, and he will give you another Helper, to be with you forever, even the Spirit of truth, whom the world cannot receive, because it neither sees him nor knows him. You know him, for he dwells with you and will be in you.

John 14:16-17

To them God chose to make known how great among the Gentiles are the riches of the glory of this mystery, which is Christ in you, the hope of glory. Him we proclaim, warning everyone and teaching everyone with all wisdom, that we may present everyone mature in Christ. For this I toil, struggling with all his energy that he powerfully works within me.

Colossians 1:27-29

Nevertheless, I tell you the truth: it is to your advantage that I go away, for if I do not go away, the Helper will not come to you. But if I go, I will send him to you. And when he comes, he will convict the world concerning sin and righteousness and judgment.

John 16:7-8

Do not be conformed to this world, but be transformed by the renewal of your mind, that by testing you may discern what is the will of God, what is good and acceptable and perfect.

Romans 12:2

Not only that, but we rejoice in our sufferings, knowing that suffering produces endurance, and endurance produces character, and character produces hope, and hope does not put us to shame, because God's love has been poured into our hearts through the Holy Spirit who has been given to us.

Romans 5:3-5

But the fruit of the Spirit is love, joy, peace, patience, kindness, goodness, faithfulness, gentleness, self-control; against such things there is no law.

Galatians 5:22-23

Count it all joy, my brothers, when you meet trials of various kinds, for you know that the testing of your faith produces steadfastness. And let steadfastness have its full effect, that you may be perfect and complete, lacking in nothing.

James 1:2-4

Go therefore and make disciples of all nations, baptizing them in the name of the Father and of the Son and of the Holy Spirit, teaching them to observe all that I have commanded you. And behold, I am with you always, to the end of the age.

Matthew 28:19-20

Hopefully you identified the amazing work that God is doing to make us more like Christ and help us live in the new realm of his kingdom. He fills us with his Spirit, he energizes us, he makes known to us his purposes and his ways, he convicts us of sin, he reveals what righteousness is like, he makes us aware of judgment to come, he makes our suffering productive, and he providentially places people in our lives who will teach us to obey him. A close look at these passages will reveal even more things God does to help us grow, and these are only a small sampling of similar verses found throughout Scripture.

Many new followers of Jesus focus only on what they need to do to grow spiritually. They ask themselves questions like, "Did I read my Bible today? Did I sin? Did I go to church?" Their entire focus is on what they are doing — or not doing. That kind of walk with God leaves them burdened with guilt and shame for not measuring up. A turning point happens in our lives when we begin to believe that God is at work to help us grow, even when we are not. As we learn to focus on what God is doing to shape our lives, our hearts fill with gratitude, and we become more convinced of God's great love for us. Knowing that God plays the essential role in our spiritual growth changes our disposition from guilt to gratitude. Spiritual growth becomes less of a burden and more of an adventure in which we experience the grace of God.

Questions for Reflection

Which of the verses describing God's activity in our spiritual lives stuck out the most to you?

_____

_____

_____

In what ways have you minimized God's role in your spiritual growth? What impact could that have on your relationship with him?

_____

_____

_____

What do you need to believe more deeply about the Holy Spirit in order to trust him for your transformation?

_____

_____

_____

What would it look like to trust more fully in his transforming work?

_____

_____

_____

Prayer

Pray through one or more of the Scriptures listed above, thanking God for the work of the Holy Spirit described in those verses. Ask him to open your eyes to see his transforming activity with a grateful heart.

SCRIPTURE MEMORY

Now after John was _____, Jesus came into Galilee, _____ the gospel of God, and saying, "The ____ is fulfilled, and the _____ of God is at hand; _____ and _____ in the gospel." –*Mark 1:14-15*

OUR PART

Scripture Study

John 15:1-8

I am the true vine, and my Father is the vinedresser. ² Every branch in me that does not bear fruit he takes away, and every branch that does bear fruit he prunes, that it may bear more fruit. ³ Already you are clean because of the word that I have spoken to you. ⁴ Abide in me, and I in you. As the branch cannot bear fruit by itself, unless it abides in the vine, neither can you, unless you abide in me. ⁵ I am the vine; you are the branches. Whoever abides in me and I in him, he it is that bears much fruit, for apart from me you can do nothing. ⁶ If anyone does not abide in me he is thrown away like a branch and withers; and the branches are gathered, thrown into the fire, and burned. ⁷ If you abide in me, and my words abide in you, ask whatever you wish, and it will be done for you. ⁸ By this my Father is glorified, that you bear much fruit and so prove to be my disciples.

Observing the Text

In this vine/branch analogy, what verbs does Jesus use to describe the branches' activity?

_____

_____

What are the two results of our bearing fruit? (v.8)

_____

_____

_____

Interpreting the Text

What does the vine analogy say about our part in our spiritual formation?

_____

_____

_____

What does it means to remain in Christ?

_____

_____

_____

Teaching

Our growth, our fruitfulness, and our transformation are completely dependent upon God. But what if we're not growing, bearing fruit, or changing? Is God to blame? Isn't he responsible to transform us?

There's a cartoon based on John 15 showing a puppet on a person's hand and captioned, _"Apart from me, you can do nothing."_ If only it were that simple. While God created us to be filled with his Spirit, he did not make us like puppets. We must learn to cooperate with him in the work of trans-formation.

We do not automatically become more like Jesus. Rather, disciples must rearrange their lives to become more like Jesus. It's something that God commands us to do.

> *But grow in the grace and knowledge of our Lord and Savior*
> *Jesus Christ.*
>
> 2 Peter 3:18a

If the Bible commands us to grow, then we bear some responsibility for our spiritual growth. But the passage does not tell us exactly what to do to grow. Instead, it focuses on two key areas of growth. The areas that he commands us to grow in inform what we can do to grow. According to the passage, we are to grow in grace and knowledge, but those answers are not the whole answer. It's the grace of our Lord and Savior Jesus Christ. It's the knowledge of our Lord and Savior Jesus Christ.

Grace is God's unmerited favor toward us that we experience in the person and work of our Lord Jesus. When we walk with Jesus, we grow deeper in our understanding of his work on our behalf. We learn to receive all of the implications of what Jesus did for us in his death on the cross, his resurrection from the dead, and his gift of great and precious promises to live by. God is commanding us to grow in our ability to understand and apply the gospel in all areas of our lives and in the lives of the people we know and love.

The knowledge of Jesus Christ is a personal knowledge. We know Jesus more because we walk with him. We listen to him. We watch him. We learn to trust him in every situation of life.

We learn to trust Jesus through pain and suffering. God uses difficulties in our lives to develop our character. Every time you forget that character development is one of God's purposes for your life, you will become frustrated by circumstances. You'll wonder, "Why is this happening to me?" or "Why am I having such a difficult time?" One answer is that life is supposed to be difficult. God uses struggles to help us grow.

Additionally, God grows people through the Bible. While we do not choose pain and suffering, we can choose to encounter God in the Bible. When you read your Bible, your Bible reads you. God speaks into the deepest parts of your life.

Where do we get our knowledge of the Lord Jesus Christ? How do we know if we are doing the things Jesus would do if he were living in our place? We know Christ in and through the scriptures. We walk with God in and through the scriptures. When we open our Bibles, God opens his mouth to speak to us.

> *For the word of God is living and active, sharper than any two-edged sword, piercing to the division of soul and of spirit, of joints and of marrow, and discerning the thoughts and intentions of the heart.*
>
> Hebrews 4:12

Because of the Bible's transformative power, Paul urges us to make it part of our everyday lives:

> *Let the word of Christ dwell in you richly, teaching and admonishing one another in all wisdom, singing psalms and hymns and spiritual songs, with thankfulness in your hearts to God.*
>
> Colossians 3:16

Scripture also encourages us over and over again to make every effort to become like Christ. In other words, our part of spiritual growth requires some effort. And while efforts do not earn our salvation, they do impact our spiritual growth. The journey of discipleship calls for effort just like studying for college, planting a crop, working out, going through counseling, giving birth, or becoming a soldier.

How much do you want to grow? Are you so eager to be transformed that you are willing to put forth significant energy and effort? It begins with a decision to devote yourself to do your part in spiritual growth.

Questions for Reflection

What do you need to do to grow in grace?

_____

_____

_____

What do you need to do to grow in the knowledge of Jesus?

_____

_____

_____

What false beliefs are stunting your growth?

_____

_____

_____

In what ways has the Bible transformed your life: your relationships, choices, thoughts? Are you regularly giving it the opportunity to do so now?

_____

_____

_____

Prayer

Praise Jesus for his goodness and grace in revealing himself to us and allowing us to know him in intimate relationship. Pray that he would give you a heart to pursue his work in your life, changing you from the inside out.

SCRIPTURE MEMORY

Now after John was arrested, _____

_____, proclaiming the

gospel of God, and saying, "____

_____

_____; _____

_____." *–Mark 1:14-15*

METAPHORS

Scripture Study

John 15:1-8

I am the true vine, and my Father is the vinedresser. ² Every branch in me that does not bear fruit he takes away, and every branch that does bear fruit he prunes, that it may bear more fruit. ³ Already you are clean because of the word that I have spoken to you. ⁴ Abide in me, and I in you. As the branch cannot bear fruit by itself, unless it abides in the vine, neither can you, unless you abide in me. ⁵ I am the vine; you are the branches. Whoever abides in me and I in him, he it is that bears much fruit, for apart from me you can do nothing. ⁶ If anyone does not abide in me he is thrown away like a branch and withers; and the branches are gathered, thrown into the fire, and burned. ⁷ If you abide in me, and my words abide in you, ask whatever you wish, and it will be done for you. ⁸ By this my Father is glorified, that you bear much fruit and so prove to be my disciples.

Observing the Text

According to verse 8, how do disciples bring glory to God?

_____

_____

_____

What actions does this passage describe God as doing?

_____

_____

_____

Interpreting the Text

How does the Father's "pruning" result in more fruit?

_____

_____

_____

In what way does our "remaining" in Christ also result in more fruit? What might this look like in our lives?

_____

_____

_____

Teaching

One of the most confusing aspects of spiritual growth is understanding how only God has the power to change our lives, but we are also held responsible for our growth. So which is it? Does God make us grow or do we make ourselves grow? A metaphor in the Bible may help us understand how God's part and our part come together.

Living in the third largest boating community in the U.S. provides opportunities for boating that desert dwellers could scarcely imagine. On one end of the spectrum are the power boats with engines that turn propellers to move the vessel through the water. On the other end are the sailboats that rely on air currents and rudders. Undoubtedly, sailing is a very different experience than powerboating. There is no diesel or gasoline to fuel a combustion engine, for their boats are powered by the wind. While sailors cannot control the wind, sailors can harness its power by setting and trimming the sails. Sailors take an active part to make it possible for the wind to power their boat, even though they have no power over the wind.

Inherently, sailors should understand one of the key principles of spiritual growth: growth requires effort, but effort does not produce the growth. The Holy Spirit is the wind that powers our growth, but we set the sails. We take an active role in receiving the work of the Holy Spirit. We make a commitment to grow when we learn to set the sails of our soul.

When Jesus spoke of the Holy Spirit, he compared the Spirit to the wind. You don't see it, but you see its effects. Actually the Greek word for spirit, *pneuma*, is also translated "wind." John 3:8 reads, *"The wind blows where it wishes, and you hear its sound, but you do not know where it comes from or where it goes. So it is with everyone who is born of the Spirit."* Becoming a Christian is a work of the Spirit of God, but we receive that work through faith. When we make the effort to set the sails, we are carried along by the wind.

That's how the Bible describes the work of the Holy Spirit when God inspired some of his followers to write the Scripture. 2 Peter 1:21 reads, *"For no prophecy was ever produced by the will of man, but men spoke from God as they were carried along by the Holy Spirit."* Instead of working with only their own power, these men were carried along by the wind of God.

We set the sails. Only God brings the wind. We are responsible to make every effort to grow, and we are completely dependent on the Holy Spirit to bring the power that makes us more like Jesus.

Questions for Reflection

What have you done to "set your sails" to receive the growth that the Holy Spirit brings? How have you seen the Spirit carry you along?

_____

_____

_____

In what ways have you minimized the work of the Spirit in you, trying instead to transform yourself without faith?

_____

_____

_____

What false beliefs do you need to repent of today, instead trusting that the Spirit works in us when we make the effort to grow?

_____

_____

_____

Prayer

Pray that the Spirit would be at work in you today, conforming you to the image of Christ. Thank him for giving you a new birth and the hope of a future glory.

WEEKLY EXERCISE

THE WORK OF THE SPIRIT

Choose one of the following exercises. Prepare to talk about it with your group.

Watch a video about setting sails. How does the video help you think about the work of the Holy Spirit in your spiritual growth?

....

Go outside where you can feel the wind on your face. Think about the ways humans harness the wind as energy. How does that relate to spiritual growth?

....

Plant something in your yard or in a pot. How does the experience of planting and nurturing the plant relate to your spiritual growth?

Get Ready for Group

Write your memorized scripture.

_____

_____

_____

_____

_____

What observations and interpretations of scripture were most meaningful
to you?

_____

_____

_____

_____

_____

Summarize your key takeaway(s) for this week.

_____

_____

_____

_____

_____

What will you tell the group about the results of your exercise this week?

_____

_____

_____

_____

_____

How has this week helped you better understand and apply the Spiritual Growth Grid?

_____

_____

_____

_____

_____

REPENT & BELIEVE

WHO GOD IS		WHAT GOD DID		WHO WE ARE		WHAT WE DO
KING	>	CALLED		CITIZENS	>	LISTEN & OBEY
FATHER	>	ADOPTED		FAMILY	>	LOVE & SERVE
SAVIOR	>	SENT		MISSIONARIES	>	GO & MULTIPLY

04

THE ROLE OF THE HOLY SPIRIT

SCRIPTURE MEMORY

And I will give you a new heart, and
a new spirit I will put within you.
And I will remove the heart of stone
from your flesh and give you a heart
of flesh. *—Ezekiel 36:26*

CREATED FOR INDWELLING

Scripture Study

John 16:4-15

But I have said these things to you, that when their hour comes you may remember that I told them to you. I did not say these things to you from the beginning, because I was with you. ⁵ But now I am going to him who sent me, and none of you asks me, "Where are you going?" ⁶ But because I have said these things to you, sorrow has filled your heart. ⁷ Nevertheless, I tell you the truth: it is to your advantage that I go away, for if I do not go away, the Helper will not come to you. But if I go, I will send him to you. ⁸ And when he comes, he will convict the world concerning sin and righteousness and judgment: ⁹ concerning sin, because they do not believe in me; ¹⁰ concerning righteousness, because I go to the Father, and you will see me no longer; 11 concerning judgment, because the ruler of this world is judged. ¹² I still have many things to say to you, but you cannot bear them now. ¹³ When the Spirit of truth comes, he will guide you into all the truth, for he will not speak on his own authority, but whatever he hears he will speak, and he will declare to you the things that are to come. ¹⁴ He will glorify me, for he will take what is mine and declare it to you. ¹⁵ All that the Father has is mine; therefore I said that he will take what is mine and declare it to you.

Observing the Text

What two names does Jesus give to the one who will come after him?

_____

_____

_____

What will the Holy Spirit do when he comes? List each verb phrase.

_____

_____

_____

Interpreting the Text

Why do you think that Jesus said, "It is to your advantage that I go away"? In what ways might the coming of the Spirit be of greater benefit than Jesus' physical presence?

_____

_____

_____

In what ways is the Holy Spirit both "the Helper" and the "Spirit of Truth"? How are those two roles different and complementary?

_____

_____

_____

Teaching

Christianity is not a set of new rules to keep. Rules can't give you power for life. So God did not give us new rules, he provided a new relationship to himself in the Holy Spirit. The Holy Spirit is not "the Force," an impersonal power, or your conscience. The Spirit is none other than God himself, the fulfillment of the promise that he would dwell in his people.

Take a deep breath. It's amazing how something so simple can make us feel relaxed and alive. The very first time a human breathed is recorded in Genesis 2:7.

The LORD God formed the man from the dust of the ground and breathed into his nostrils the breath of life, and the man became a living being.

But man is not just a living being; man is a spiritual being. In the biblical languages, both Hebrew and Greek, the word used for "spirit" is also used for breath. In Hebrew, it's the word *ruach*. God's plan is for the breath of God to be in man, giving life in every moment through the presence of his Spirit.

From the beginning, we were created to live in dependence on God and in continual fellowship with him. Human beings were created to be fully alive in the Garden of Eden. Then sin came, and spiritual death came with it. When man sinned, dependence on the Holy Spirit to give life was lost. We were cut off and spiritually dead. But God began to unfold a plan to restore life in the Spirit, which means human beings can now live every moment of every day being filled with the Holy Spirit of God.

In the Old Testament, the Spirit of God came "on" certain people at certain times in certain places to give special insights, strengths, or guidance. This

Spirit accompanied Moses as a cloud by day and a fire by night to lead the children of Israel through the Exodus (Exodus 13:21). The Spirit came upon Samson to give him strength beyond any other man (Judges 6:12 & 14:6). Ezekiel was filled with the Spirit of the Lord in order to prophesy God's words to his people (Ezekiel 11:5).

God also promised his Spirit to come upon the community of his people. Ezekiel 37 tells of a valley of dry bones, an allegory about Israel. The dead, dry bones come together, but there is still no breath in them. Then God tells Ezekiel to speak to the bones.

> Then he said to me, "Prophesy to the breath; prophesy, son of man, and say to the breath, Thus says the LORD GOD: Come from the four winds, O breath, and breathe on these slain, that they may live." So I prophesied as he commanded me, and the breath came into them, and they lived and stood on their feet, an exceedingly great army... And I will put my Spirit within you, and you shall live, and I will place you in your own land. Then you shall know that I am the LORD; I have spoken, and I will do it, declares the LORD."
>
> Ezekiel 37:9-10, 14

God gave his people a similar promise in the previous chapter.

> And I will give you a new heart, and a new spirit I will put within you. And I will remove the heart of stone from your flesh and give you a heart of flesh.
>
> Ezekiel 36:26

God's people got a taste of a promise that would ultimately come to all his people, and would be fulfilled on the day of Pentecost. God put his Spirit in his people. In the Old Testament, the Spirit of God came on people, but it was temporary and not on everyone. God promised that one day all of that would change. Through the prophet Joel, God said,

> *And it shall come to pass afterward,*
> *that I will pour out my Spirit on all flesh;*
> *your sons and your daughters shall prophesy,*
> *your old men shall dream dreams,*
> *and your young men shall see visions.*
> *Even on the male and female servants*
> *in those days I will pour out my Spirit.*
>
> Joel 2:28-29

God promised that he would pour out his Spirit on all his people, no matter their rank or social status, age, or gender. This became the great dream of the people of Israel.

In the New Testament, Jesus compared the Holy Spirit to streams of living water that would bring refreshment, satisfaction, and unending life to the people of God (John 7:37-39).

In John 20, the disciples of Jesus are locked away for fear of their lives. The crucified Jesus appeared to them to give them a preview of the day when the Holy Spirit would come on all of God's people.

> *Jesus said to them again, "Peace be with you. As the Father*
> *has sent me, even so I am sending you." And when he had said*
> *this, he breathed on them and said to them, "Receive the Holy*
> *Spirit."*
>
> John 20:21-22

This passage should remind us of God's original creation of Adam, when he formed him from the dust and breathed life into his lungs. The Greek verb breathed is only used here in the New Testament. But the Old Testament translated into Greek (known as the Septuagint or abbreviated as LXX) uses this same phrase in Genesis 2:7. Jesus wanted his disciples to know that when they received the Holy Spirit, it would be the Spirit of Jesus in them. The same life-giving breath that initiated human life is the true source of spiritual vitality.

Finally, we see the promise fulfilled in Acts 2, when the Holy Spirit comes on the day of Pentecost. The Apostle Peter reminded the crowd that this event was what the Old Testament prophet Joel was talking about.

Just as God resurrected the dry bones, he will give new life to you. Just as Jesus breathed on his disciples, he will breathe on you. This is the promise of the Holy Spirit. Like a body needs to be indwelt by life-giving oxygen to fulfill its purpose, we were made to be indwelt by the Holy Spirit.

Questions for Reflection

How has this study shifted your thinking about who the Holy Spirit is and the work he accomplishes? In what ways have you struggled to see him as an active presence in your life?

_____

_____

_____

How do you need to give a greater focus in your life on the work of the Holy Spirit in and through you?

_____

_____

_____

What false beliefs about the Holy Spirit's nature have distorted your responses to him?

_____

_____

_____

Prayer

Praise our three-in-one God who created, saved, and now indwells us. Thank him for filling us and giving us life — not just a few believers, but all of us; not just for a moment, but forever.

SCRIPTURE MEMORY

And I will give you a _____, and

a new spirit I will put within you.

And I will remove the _____

from your flesh and give you a heart

of flesh. *—Ezekiel 36:26*

EMPOWERED BY THE HOLY SPIRIT

Scripture Study

John 14:16-17

And I will ask the Father, and he will give you another Helper, to be with you forever, [17] even the Spirit of truth, whom the world cannot receive, because it neither sees him nor knows him. You know him, for he dwells with you and will be in you.

Observing the Text

What two names are given to the Holy Spirit in this passage?

_____

_____

_____

According to this passage, where will the Spirit come to live?

_____

_____

_____

Interpreting the Text

How are the persons of the Trinity described in this passage?

_____

_____

_____

How does the Spirit's proximity to us result in us knowing him?

_____

_____

_____

Teaching

On Day 1 of this lesson, we learned that the Holy Spirit indwells followers of Jesus. He gives spiritual life to us in the same way that breath gives life to our bodies. Breathe in. Breathe out. Feel the refreshment of every breath in your body. Now, by faith, breathe in the Holy Spirit.

Jesus said that his followers need the Holy Spirit so much that they were to wait for the Holy Spirit to come before they even tried to live the Christian life or take part in Jesus' mission.

> *And while staying with them he ordered them not to depart from Jerusalem, but to wait for the promise of the Father, which, he said, "you heard from me; for John baptized with water, but you will be baptized with the Holy Spirit not many days from now."*
>
> Acts 1:4-5

Without the power of the Holy Spirit filling our lives, we don't have what it takes to live as a Christian. I (Bruce) learned this lesson the hard way. One of the spiritual markers of my life happened in Abilene, Texas in June 1980. At age 19, I was serious about my faith in Jesus. I was trying really hard to keep the Christian rules, as I understood them, but I was failing over and again. My constant struggle with sin frustrated me. But what made things worse was that I believed the Christian life was something I was supposed to do. I thought that if I loved God, I would live a holy life and I would break my bad habits. But I was unable to get control of my life. I became so weary and frustrated with my efforts that I was ready to quit the faith. That's when I read *The Key to Triumphant Living*, a book based on the truth in Colossians 1:27.

> *To them God chose to make known how great among the Gentiles are the riches of the glory of this mystery, which is Christ in you, the hope of glory.*

The hope of glory is Christ in you. In other words, the only way that we are able to live the Christian life as God intended is when we understand that the power to live the Christian life comes from Christ in us. The indwelling Holy Spirit is the key.

In an apartment in Abilene, I first understood the role of the Holy Spirit in my life. One of the most important discoveries of my life was learning to depend on the indwelling Holy Spirit to give me power beyond myself. For the first time, I began to breathe in and breathe out. I began to experience the power of the Holy Spirit in my life.

Jesus described the role of the Holy Spirit to his disciples on the night he was betrayed. He took time to prepare them for his departure. He would no longer be with them. What were they to do without his leadership and guidance?

Nevertheless, I tell you the truth: it is to your advantage that I go away, for if I do not go away, the Helper will not come to you. But if I go, I will send him to you.

John 16:7

How could it be good that Jesus was going away? For three years, their lives were wrapped up in the life of Jesus. They left everything to follow him, and now he tells them he's about to leave. How could that be to their advantage? But Jesus knew that unless he went away, the Helper — the Holy Spirit — would not come.

Sometimes I think I would love to have lived in the time when I could have seen Jesus on the earth. Wouldn't that have been amazing? But Jesus says it is better to live in the age of the Spirit than during the time when he was on the earth. We are more fortunate than his disciples because we can enjoy the unlimited presence of God through the Holy Spirit.

And I will ask the Father, and he will give you another Helper, to be with you forever, even the Spirit of truth, whom the world cannot receive, because it neither sees him nor knows him. You know him, for he dwells with you and will be in you.

John 14:16-17

The Spirit is another *Helper.* The same word is sometimes translated, counselor. Jesus said the Holy Spirit dwells in us, and he will help us forever as our counselor.

Something happens in the presence of a counselor. You receive wisdom and insight. You get clarity about what is going on in your heart. You learn the truth about yourself and receive guidance for daily living. Being with a counselor is a safe place where you can disclose the truth about your life. And if the counselor is good, you experience the healing power of acceptance and grace.

After seeing a counselor, we go back to our lives. But wouldn't it be great if the counselor could go with us? What if the counselor could be there when we talk to our children or when we need to know the right thing to say at the office? The Holy Spirit is the counselor who is always with us.

But the Bible says the Holy Spirit does more than serve as our counselor:

He reveals Jesus to us (John 15:26).

He convicts us of sin and our need for God (John 16:8-11).

He gives us confidence that we are God's children (Romans 8:16).

He empowers our witness for Jesus (Acts 1:8).

He guides us in life (Romans 8:14).

He gives us courage (2 Timothy 1:7).

He gifts us to serve God and others (1 Corinthians 12:7-11).

He gives us hope when we have lost hope (Romans 15:13).

He shows us how to reconcile a relationship (Galatians 6:1).

He strengthens us to follow God's leadings (Ephesians 3:14-16).

He empowers us to overcome temptation (Galatians 5:16).

He helps us understand the scripture (1 Corinthians 2:11-13).

He enables us to demonstrate godly character (Galatians 5:22-23).

He helps us express ourselves to God in prayer (Romans 8:26-27).

We don't need to have all the answers to the issues and problems in our lives. Instead, everything we need to do to be a fully devoted follower of Jesus can be done through the power of the Holy Spirit.

Questions for Reflection

In what ways do you try to accomplish the behavior of the Christian life on your own, rather than in dependence on the Spirit?

_____

_____

_____

How have you seen the Spirit actively working in your life? What does that look like?

_____

_____

_____

When we fail to depend on the Spirit's power, we reveal a false belief in our ability to accomplish our own salvation. Do you need to repent of trying to live the Christian life in your own power? Take a moment to acknowledge your need for him today.

_____

_____

_____

Prayer

Ask the Holy Spirit to fill you with his power to live the Christian life. Pray for his counsel, courage, and character to guide and grow in you as you look to him for help.

SCRIPTURE MEMORY

And I will give you a new heart, and
a _____ I will _____.
And I will _____ the heart of stone
from your flesh and give you a _____
_____. –*Ezekiel 36:26*

WALK IN THE SPIRIT

Scripture Study

Galatians 5:16-26

But I say, walk by the Spirit, and you will not gratify the desires of the flesh. [17] For the desires of the flesh are against the Spirit, and the desires of the Spirit are against the flesh, for these are opposed to each other, to keep you from doing the things you want to do. [18] But if you are led by the Spirit, you are not under the law. [19] Now the works of the flesh are evident: sexual immorality, impurity, sensuality, [20] idolatry, sorcery, enmity, strife, jealousy, fits of anger, rivalries, dissensions, divisions, [21] envy, drunkenness, orgies, and things like these. I warn you, as I warned you before, that those who do such things will not inherit the kingdom of God. [22] But the fruit of the Spirit is love, joy, peace, patience, kindness, goodness, faithfulness, [23] gentleness, self-control; against such things there is no law. [24] And those who belong to Christ Jesus have crucified the flesh with its passions and desires. [25] If we live by the Spirit, let us also keep in step with the Spirit. [26] Let us not become conceited, provoking one another, envying one another.

Observing the Text

What is the result of walking by the Spirit?

_____

_____

_____

What four verb phrases are used in this passage to describe our interaction with the Spirit?

_____

_____

_____

Interpreting the Text

In what ways are the desires of the flesh and the desires of the Spirit opposed to each other?

_____

_____

_____

How does dependence on the Spirit lead to the growth of the fruit described in verses 22-23?

_____

_____

_____

Teaching

When it comes to the topic of the Holy Spirit, confusion abounds. What is the baptism of the Spirit? What does it mean to be filled with the Spirit? How do we walk by the Spirit? The way people answer these questions often hints at what church they belong to. For clarity, definitions of each will help.

The **baptism of the Holy Spirit** happens at salvation. When someone places his or her faith in Jesus, the Holy Spirit indwells that person, and that believer is sealed by the Holy Spirit. There is no such thing as a Christian who does not have the baptism of the Holy Spirit (Acts 2:38, Ephesians 1:13, Romans 8:9).

The **filling of the Holy Spirit**, or fullness of the Spirit, happens repeatedly as one surrenders to the control of the Holy Spirit in all things. Believers are commanded to be filled with the Holy Spirit continually (Ephesians 5:18). We will focus on being filled with the Holy Spirit in week 5.

To **walk by the Spirit** is similar to being filled with the Holy Spirit; they are two sides of the same coin. To be filled with the Spirit is passive — only God can fill us. To walk by the Spirit is active — we act in faith based on our beliefs about the Spirit and in response to the Holy Spirit.

So, if the Holy Spirit indwells and empowers followers of Jesus, is it possible to be indwelt by the Holy Spirit and not live in the power of the Holy Spirit? Yes, that's why the New Testament directs believers to walk by the Spirit. *"If we live by the Spirit, let us also keep in step with the Spirit"* (Galatians 5:25).

We experience the power of the Holy Spirit when we keep in step with the Spirit, staying close to him. When he moves, we move. We follow each prompting of the Spirit.

In his book, *Classic Christianity*, Bob George paints a helpful image of the difference between trying to live the Christian life in your own power and walking by the Spirit.

Imagine yourself in a large house, in which are living both deaf and hearing people. They are all mixed together. You can't tell by looking who is deaf and who is hearing. Sitting in a room by himself is a man. As you watch, you notice that he is tapping his toes rhythmically and snapping his fingers in time. You know what is happening. He is listening to music and obviously enjoying himself. His whole body wants to respond to what his ears are receiving. There is nothing strange or mysterious about it.

But now, let's add a new person to the scene. One of the deaf persons opens the door and enters the room. He immediately sees the first man and walks over to him and smiles a greeting. The deaf man watches the music lover for a few moments. The deaf man thinks to himself, "He sure seems to be enjoying himself, I think I'll give it a try."

So the deaf man sits next to the first man and begins to imitate him. Awkwardly and haltingly at first, he tries to snap his fingers, tap his toes and move like the person next to him. Everybody has some sense of rhythm, whether they can hear or not. After a little practice, the deaf man is snapping and tapping in time with the first man. He even smiles a little bit and shrugs, "It's not that much fun, but I guess it's OK."

Let's now add a final person to the story. A third man walks into the room, what does he see? Two men apparently doing the same thing. But is there a difference? Absolutely. All the difference in the world. The first man's actions are natural responses to the music he hears. The deaf man is only imitating those outward actions. Even though he can't hear a note. That is the difference between real Christianity and legalism.

When we are approaching God in the way he intends, our attitudes and actions are a response to the music we hear. That music is a personal relationship with the living Christ whose Spirit indwells those who have faith in him. It's the music of a trust relationship with God in every matter of life.

On the other hand, a legalist could not care less if you are stone deaf to the love and grace of God. Legalism is just about getting people to snap and tap at the right time.[1]

In this illustration, Bob George pictures someone who walks by the Spirit and someone who does not. They might look alike at any given moment, but they are very different. The difference is not their activity in the moment but what is driving the activity – the leading of the Holy Spirit.

But how does the Spirit lead? He leads us through scripture, teaching, wise counsel, the declaration of the glory of God in nature, and promptings that come to us personally but may defy explanation. Thus, to walk by the Spirit, we listen to the Spirit and act in faith as a response to him.

When we disobey, we no longer walk by the Spirit. We are not keeping in step with him. Rather, we grieve the Holy Spirit (Ephesians 4:30) and quench the Holy Spirit (1 Thessalonians 5:19).

We were created to be indwelt by God himself. The coming of the Holy Spirit at Pentecost is the fulfillment of God's promise to indwell his people. The Holy Spirit empowers followers of Jesus to receive God's promises and obey his commands. So we must learn to walk by the Spirit, instead of depending on our own power, to overcome sin and keep God's law.

---

1 Bob George, *Classic Christianity* (Eugene, OR: Harvest House, 1989), 152-53.

Questions for Reflection

How have you experienced the Spirit's guidance? What are the primary ways that he has led you?

_____

_____

_____

Why is it difficult to tell the difference between someone depending on the Spirit and someone who is living in their own strength?

_____

_____

_____

In what ways do you see unbelief and disobedience grieving the Holy Spirit and quenching his work in your life? Examine your heart and repent of any unwillingness to depend on his strength and guidance.

_____

_____

_____

Prayer

Thank the Spirit for his continual indwelling and overcoming power. Ask for his guidance and the strength to follow wherever he leads.

WEEKLY
EXERCISE

PRACTICING DEPENDENCE

Over the next few days, practice actively depending on the Spirit in some area of your life. This could be a particular relationship (like your spouse or a co-worker), an area of struggle (maybe your morning commute), or a task in which you need to work in the Spirit's power and not your own.

So what does active dependence look like, practically speaking?

Like the deaf man tapping his foot, working in our own strength may look identical to Spirit-led behavior. However, our motivation and mindset will be vastly different. John Piper uses the acronym APTAT to set his thinking in a direction of working in the Spirit's power and not his own. Try using this acronym in the area you've chosen, and be prepared to share with your group how your beliefs and behavior were impacted.

> A - I acknowledge that without Christ I can do nothing (John 15:5; Romans 7:18).
>
> P - I pray that God would make me love as Jesus loves, and work in me all that is pleasing to him (1 Thessalonians 2:12; Romans 5:21; Hebrews 13:21).
>
> T - I trust the promise of God's help and strength and guid ance (Isaiah 41:10; James 1:5, 6).
>
> A - I act in obedience to God's word (Philippians 2:12)
>
> T - I thank God for whatever good comes I give him the glory (1 Peter 4:11).[2]

You will need a helper with this exercise—your child, your spouse or a friend. Blindfold yourself and ask your helper to guide you to go from sit-

2 Adapted from John Piper, https://www.desiringgod.org/articles/dana-doug-and-an-ap-tat-recap.

ting in your favorite spot in the living room to carry out the trash. Your helper cannot touch you or move anything around you. They can only speak instructions to you. No peeking. Be careful. In addition, write a waiver of all legal liabilities for any of the authors of this material. Sign it. Now do this exercise.

Reflect on the experience. How did you feel? What did the experience require of you? What did it require of your helper? What do you think the implications are for walking in the Spirit?

Get Ready for Group

Write your memorized scripture.

_____
_____
_____
_____
_____

What observations and interpretations of scripture were most meaningful to you?

_____
_____
_____
_____
_____

Summarize your key takeaway(s) for this week.

_____
_____
_____
_____
_____

What will you tell the group about the results of your exercise this week?

_____
_____
_____
_____
_____

How has this week helped you better understand and apply the Spiritual Growth Grid?

_____

_____

_____

_____

_____

05

BE FILLED WITH THE HOLY SPIRIT

SCRIPTURE MEMORY

And do not get drunk with wine, for
that is debauchery, but be filled with
the Spirit. –*Ephesians 5:18*

HOW TO GET DRUNK AND STAY DRUNK

Scripture Study

Ephesians 5:15-21

Look carefully then how you walk, not as unwise but as wise,16 making the best use of the time, because the days are evil. ⁷ Therefore do not be foolish, but understand what the will of the Lord is. ¹⁸ And do not get drunk with wine, for that is debauchery, but be filled with the Spirit, ¹⁹ addressing one another in psalms and hymns and spiritual songs, singing and making melody to the Lord with your heart,²⁰ giving thanks always and for everything to God the Father in the name of our Lord Jesus Christ, ²¹ submitting to one another out of reverence for Christ.

Observing the Text

List the positive commands given in this passage.

_____

_____

_____

List the negative commands given in this passage.

_____

_____

Interpreting the Text

List the three direct contrasts you see in this passage. What can we learn from these negative and positive counterparts?

_____

_____

_____

In what way is verse 18 not only a contrast but also a comparison?

_____

_____

_____

Teaching

We begin this week with a brief review. The Spiritual Growth Grid is based on an understanding that repentance is a way of life, and identity informs activity. To repent means we change our way of thinking, and we reconsider our strategy for living. In effect, we rearrange our life and activities around a new way of thinking about God and ourselves. It's the only way we experience real change.

Obedience is the outcome of living a life where we repent and believe. We all feel the need to change. But how does real change come? Spiritual transformation includes both God's activity and our own. God's part is primarily carried out by the Holy Spirit. In Week 4, we learned that the Holy Spirit indwells followers of Jesus when they place their faith in Jesus.

Only the Holy Spirit can give us the power to live as a Christian, so we must learn to walk by the Spirit.

This week, we will learn what followers of Jesus do to be filled with the Holy Spirit. Last week we gave you this definition: *the filling of the Holy Spirit happens repeatedly as one surrenders to the control of the Holy Spirit in all things. Believers are commanded to be filled with the Holy Spirit continually.*

The church I (Bruce) attended as a young Christian said little about the Holy Spirit. Their focus was the Father, the Son, and the Holy Bible. But repeatedly, the Bible shows us that the power for living the Christian life is found in the Holy Spirit of God. So how do we relate to the Holy Spirit in a way that we experience God and his power? That's what Ephesians 5:18 is all about. *"And do not get drunk with wine, for that is debauchery, but be filled with the Spirit."*

Paul introduces a new metaphor in this verse. We've talked about the Holy Spirit as breath, wind, and living water. In this verse, he talks about alcohol to help us understand how to be filled with the Spirit.

Some say, "Do not get drunk with wine? No problem! I only drink beer." But Paul's metaphor is not specific to wine; it's drunkenness. While there are many warnings about alcohol in the Bible, alcohol is not forbidden. But drunkenness is. First, it's excessive, then it's destructive. Drunkenness means surrendering control to something outside yourself. Only people who get drunk become a drunk. So the Bible commands us, "do not get drunk with wine".

In the same verse, he says we are to be filled with the Holy Spirit. Why? Is he contrasting the negative behavior of drunkenness with the positive behavior of being filled with the Holy Spirit? Maybe in part, but that's not the main point.

The apostle Paul speaks of drunkenness as a comparison to being filled with the Holy Spirit. So in order to understand what we don't know about the filling of the Holy Spirit, we should think about what we do know about drunkenness.

When I lived in Cut-N-Shoot, Texas, I served as the Student Pastor. I was taking some students home from an event one night when I came upon a young man lying in the middle of the road. When I stopped to check on him, I rolled down my window. He reached up with both hands to grasp the driver-side door, then pulled himself up until we were face-to-face, only inches apart. I smelled a strong mix of alcohol and sweat, and I recognized him. When he realized I was a pastor at his church, he said, "I am not who you think I am."

I have laughed at his response ever since that night. Yet, he was right: at least in one sense he was not who I thought he was. He was a different person that night because he let alcohol take control of him. And when alcohol took control, he acted in ways I had never seen him act before.

We know excessive drinking makes you drunk. We know repetitive drunkenness creates dependence. We know drunkenness is destructive. We know drunkenness changes your behavior. It's powerful that way. So we compare drunkenness to being filled with the Holy Spirit, not in the sense that being filled with the Holy Spirit is destructive, but in the sense that both have the power to create a dependence that changes us.

To be filled with the Holy Spirit is to be under the control of the Holy Spirit. It is to develop a dependence upon him that changes us for the better.

Questions for Reflection

Do you regularly pray to be filled with the Spirit, surrendering to his control? Why or why not?

_____

_____

How might dependence on the Holy Spirit affect your decision making, priorities, relationships, and behavior?

_____

_____

_____

What are you dependent on? For example, our sinful nature urges us to depend on our own competence, wealth, ability, appearance, relationships, career, etc.

_____

_____

_____

What does our struggle to depend on the Spirit's power reveal about what we truly believe?

_____

_____

_____

Prayer

Ask the Spirit of Truth to fill you today, surrendering your control to follow him. Pray that he would empower you to walk in his ways and guide you into the knowledge of truth.

SCRIPTURE MEMORY

And do not get _____ with wine, for

that is debauchery, but be _____ with

the _____. —*Ephesians 5:18*

GRAMMAR MATTERS

Scripture Study

Ephesians 5:15-21

Look carefully then how you walk, not as unwise but as wise,16 making the best use of the time, because the days are evil. [17] Therefore do not be foolish, but understand what the will of the Lord is. [18] And do not get drunk with wine, for that is debauchery, but be filled with the Spirit, [19] addressing one another in psalms and hymns and spiritual songs, singing and making melody to the Lord with your heart,20 giving thanks always and for every-thing to God the Father in the name of our Lord Jesus Christ, [21] submitting to one another out of reverence for Christ.

Observing the Text

How many members of the Trinity are mentioned in this passage?

_____

_____

_____

List the behaviors that result from the filling of the Spirit (verses 19-21).

_____

_____

Interpreting the Text

Why do you think Paul listed these specific behaviors when he describes the life of dependence on the Spirit?

_____

_____

_____

Which of the members of the Trinity is most active in these verses? What is he doing that we can't do for ourselves?

_____

_____

_____

Teaching

On Day 1, we saw how the Apostle Paul compared drunkenness to being filled with the Holy Spirit. Just like a person can be under the control of alcohol and act in ways he or she did not act before, a person can be under the control of the Holy Spirit and act in ways he or she did not act before.

Thinking about drunkenness is not the only way to understand this verse. We also need a lesson in grammar to fully understand being filled with the Holy Spirit. The phrase, "Be filled with the Spirit" is known as a Present Passive Imperative. We'll break that down into parts.

Present Tense: calls for continuous action

Passive Voice: the subject is acted upon

Imperative Mood: a command to assert the will

So let's apply the nuances to the simple phrase, _be filled with the Spirit_.

Present Tense: Paul is emphasizing continuous action. We must keep on being filled with the Holy Spirit. This isn't just a one-time event that happened in the past.

Passive Voice: Being filled with the Spirit isn't something we do. It's done to us. We are the ones being acted upon. Only God can fill us with the Spirit. We are dependent on him.

Imperative Mood: This phrase is a command. We must assert the will to do it, even though we cannot fill ourselves with the Holy Spirit. Therefore, we are called to act in a way that places us in a position for God to fill us with his Spirit.

The metaphor of drunkenness demonstrated that being filled with the Holy Spirit is about *living in dependence* on the Spirit so that we are under his control. The grammar gives us better insight into how we depend on the Spirit in three specific ways. In this lesson, we consider one of the three insights. We will examine the other two insights in the next lesson.

To be filled with the Holy Spirit we live in continuous dependence. This aspect of dependence is all about time. We keep on being filled every moment of every day. We surrender at all times. We surrendered our life to the Lordship of Jesus in the past, and we continuously surrender to his Lordship moment by moment and day by day.

In the language of the New Testament, remember how Spirit and breath are the same word. To stay alive, we must continue to breathe. If we stop breathing, even for a relatively short period of time, we die.

When I (Bruce) was sixteen years old, I played a game at summer camp that involved two teams of teenagers, a swimming pool, and a watermelon that had Vaseline all over it. The object was for one team of about thirty people to get the melon out on one end of the pool, while the other team of thirty tried to get the melon out on the other end.

I was aggressive enough to get my hands all over the watermelon. But the problem was that every time I got near the melon, people pushed me under water. It did not take long for me to realize that there was something more important than the watermelon — air.

At one point in the contest, with everyone fighting for the melon, no one noticed that I was pushed under the water by the throng of bodies and could not get to the surface. I could see the watermelon on the surface of the water, and I knew that above it was the air I needed so badly. But I could not get to the air! I legitimately thought I was going to die. I thought, "This is going to make the evening news, and it's going to ruin this whole week of youth camp." I wanted a breath of air more than anything in the world, and I realized I had taken for granted all those years of breathing freely.

Although I could not get to the surface, I did manage to get my arm out of the water in an effort to reach the side of the pool. That's when someone grabbed my hand and yanked me completely out of the water. I got what I longed for! I took a deep, heaving breath of life-giving air. And another. And another. The oxygen filled my lungs, the red blood cells did their job, and my body began to function again as a living thing. And after a few minutes, I had more strength.

When we want the Holy Spirit to empower our life as desperately as a drowning man wants air to give life to his body, we must turn to God and ask him to fill us with his Holy Spirit. We will realize that all the metaphorical greased melons we've known are not worth missing the breath of God. Having the Spirit of God is the only way to experience the life God intended. We don't need him occasionally. We need him continuously. We need him desperately.

Being filled with the Holy Spirit is not a spectacular experience that happens one time in your history. Rather, it's an ongoing process of surrendering to the Holy Spirit daily. With that said, even lifelong processes must have a beginning.

Start today. Practice being aware of the Holy Spirit in every moment: when you get angry, when you are tired, and when you are about to say something that a person filled with the Holy Spirit would not say.

But remember we cannot do this on our own. Before we even try, let's ask God to fill us right now. And at the first sign that we have started to sober up or run out of breath, we must ask again.

> *If you then, who are evil, know how to give good gifts to your children, how much more will the heavenly Father give the Holy Spirit to those who ask him!*
>
> Luke 11:13

> *O God, you are my God; earnestly I seek you;*
> *my soul thirsts for you;*
> *my flesh faints for you,*
> *as in a dry and weary land where there is no water.*
>
> Psalm 63:1

Questions for Reflection

What does this emphasis on continuous dependence reveal about God's desire for a relationship with his people?

_____

_____

_____

What difference would it make if you approached your relationships, job, finances, ambitions, etc. while continuously depending on the Holy Spirit?

_____

_____

_____

Our culture in America values independence. Admitting your dependence is counterintuitive to our Do-It-Yourself mindset. In what ways are your beliefs more shaped by our cultural priorities than by the truth in Scripture?

_____

_____

_____

Prayer

Praise God that he is continuously dependable. He is eternally worthy of our trust and faithful to his promises. Pray that he would fill you with his Spirit as you surrender to his Lordship.

SCRIPTURE MEMORY

And do not get _____, for

that is debauchery, but _____

_____. *—Ephesians 5:18*

DAY
3

DYING AND RELYING

Scripture Study

Ephesians 5:15-21

Look carefully then how you walk, not as unwise but as wise, ¹⁶ making the best use of the time, because the days are evil. ¹⁷ Therefore do not be foolish, but understand what the will of the Lord is. ¹⁸ And do not get drunk with wine, for that is debauchery, but be filled with the Spirit, ¹⁹ addressing one another in psalms and hymns and spiritual songs, singing and making melody to the Lord with your heart, ²⁰ giving thanks always and for every-thing to God the Father in the name of our Lord Jesus Christ, ²¹ submitting to one another out of reverence for Christ.

Observing the Text

What is *therefore* in verse 17 pointing back to?

_____

_____

_____

What other positive command is paired with "be filled with the Spirit" as a result of the *therefore* in verse 17?

_____

_____

_____

Interpreting the Text

What relationship can you see between the two positive commands in verses 17-18?

_____

_____

_____

In this passage, how does being filled with the Spirit result in glory for the Trinity as a whole?

_____

_____

_____

Ephesians 5:18 commands us to be filled with the Holy Spirit. In this verse, the apostle used a metaphor of drunkenness to show that being filled with the Holy Spirit is about *living in dependence on the Spirit* so that we are under his control. The grammar used in the passage gives us better insight into *how we depend on the Spirit*. The apostle spoke of three ways we depend on the Holy Spirit who indwells us.

We saw on Day 2 that we must practice continuous dependence on the Holy Spirit, surrendering at all times, moment by moment. Today, we see two more ways we depend on the Holy Spirit.

To be filled with the Spirit means we live in complete dependence on him. We are not just influenced by the Holy Spirit; we are filled with him. There's a vast difference between being influenced by the Spirit and being filled with the Spirit.

As previously stated, the command in Ephesians 5:18 is in the passive voice, which means we are not the ones who do the filling but the ones acted upon. We cannot fill ourselves. Only God can fill us. So, what do we do to put ourselves in a position where God will fill us?

We must empty ourselves. If we are filled with ourselves, we cannot be filled with the Holy Spirit. One aspect of being filled with the Holy Spirit is to submit every area of our life to God. If some area of our life is not surrendered to the Holy Spirit, we are, by definition, not being filled with the Holy Spirit. After all, we are not empty of ourselves. He might be present, but he is not in complete control of our life until we choose to surrender all of our life to him.

We do not need more of the Holy Spirit. Rather, we need to surrender more of ourselves to the Holy Spirit. The Bible and Christians throughout history speak of surrendering ourselves to the Holy Spirit as dying to ourselves. We do not seek to be large and in charge, but we empty ourselves so he can fill us. We die to our life so that we might be filled with his life. It's difficult, but it's the only way to be filled with the Holy Spirit.

In John 12, Jesus knew he was approaching the cross where he would suffer for our sins. Speaking to his disciples, he compared himself to a seed that must be planted in the ground and lose itself in the earth before it can become the plant that grows into a stalk and bears much fruit. He said that we die to live.

> *Truly, truly, I say to you, unless a grain of wheat falls into the earth and dies, it remains alone; but if it dies, it bears much fruit.*
>
> John 12:24

Later in the Bible, Paul reinforces this idea with his own testimony of how he had to die in order to experience the life of Christ.

I have been crucified with Christ. It is no longer I who live, but Christ who lives in me. And the life I now live in the flesh I live by faith in the Son of God, who loved me and gave himself for me.

Galatians 2:20

The reason we may struggle to live in the power of the Holy Spirit is because, unlike Paul, we have not decided that it's *no longer I who live.*

As a woman sat at our kitchen table considering whether to become a Christian, she said, "I want this life with God. I want to trust in Jesus and be filled with his Spirit." Then she added, "I want to do this, but I'm afraid God might make me weird." (Secretly, I wondered if this worried her because she thought I was weird.)

She is not alone. Others might say, "I'm afraid if I live in complete dependence on God and the Holy Spirit fills my life that God will make me..." Fill in the blank. Some may fear that God will make them poor, passive, weak, bigoted, obnoxious or any number of other undesirable traits.

Are you afraid of what God will make you become if you die to yourself and surrender every aspect of your life to God? Are you concerned that you might not like the person God makes you to be?

For the record, here's what God says he will make us to become. God will make us free. *"Where the Spirit of the Lord is, there is freedom"* (2 Corinthians 3:17). And he will make us loving (Galatians 5:22). Being free and being loving are what awaits us on the other side of dying to ourselves and being filled with the Holy Spirit.

Here's the deal, no one is accidentally filled with the Holy Spirit. We decide to be filled. Ephesians 5:18 is an imperative, which means it's a command. So we consciously depend on the Holy Spirit to bring power into our life that we don't have.

Note that the verse does not say we are filled *by* the Spirit. He is not on the outside, giving us what we need. We are filled *with* the Spirit. He is what we need. We don't need him to just give us patience. He is our patience. We don't need him to make us loving. We need him to be loving through us.

I (Bruce) experienced this when my wife and I were hurt deeply by someone. It was a heartbreaking betrayal. We struggled against our anger turning into bitterness, and then our bitterness turning into hate. We knew the right answer was to forgive. I tried to forgive, but my pride wanted revenge more than forgiveness. I became aware of my inability to forgive, and I became conscious of God's grace. I needed him to do inside of me what I could not do. So instead of asking God to help me, I became consciously dependent on the Holy Spirit's power to forgive. I acknowledged, "God, I can't forgive this hurt, but you are really good at forgiving. I want your forgiveness to well up in me." It didn't happen overnight, but like healing after surgery, each day got a little better. I can relate to the prayer of hymn-writer Andrew Reed:

> Holy Spirit, all divine,
> Dwell within this heart of mine;
> Cast down every idol throne,
> Reign supreme, and reign alone.

We are commanded by God to be filled with his Holy Spirit. His plan is for us to be empowered by the Spirit through continual, complete, and conscious dependence on him in all of life.

Ask God to fill you with his Spirit. Try praying this brief prayer multiple times a day, especially when you are aware of your own selfish interests: "Lord, it is no longer I who live but Christ who lives in me. I die to myself. Please fill me with your Holy Spirit." And believe by faith that God has heard you.

Questions for Reflection

In what areas of your life are you still clinging to control? How would it make a difference if you surrendered those areas today?

_____

_____

_____

What is the difference between asking for help to change and asking the Spirit to do the work in our place?

_____

_____

_____

What false belief is revealed when we see the Spirit as someone who fills us with what we need, rather than the one who is filling us with himself? How can correcting this belief change the way we pray and obey?

_____

_____

_____

Prayer

Pray that the Spirit would grow your dependence to be continuous, complete, and conscious. Acknowledge your need to die to yourself and ask him to fill you today.

WEEKLY EXERCISE

BEING FILLED WITH THE SPIRIT

This exercise will prepare you to be filled with the Holy Spirit through prayer. Remember, the filling of the Holy Spirit is a command from God. We need God's power to live the Christian life.

Remind yourself of the following passage. Then pray according to the four prompts below. Take your time. Do not rush this.

> *If you then, who are evil, know how to give good gifts to your children, how much more will the heavenly Father give the Holy Spirit to those who ask him!*
>
> Luke 11:13

1. Surrender the control of your life to God's Spirit in prayer.

You might pray, "Father, I surrender completely the control of my life to you." Be specific about the areas of your life that you tend to hold back from God. For example, you might pray, "God, I surrender my work to you. I want you to be in control of all of my work, my relationships at work, the decisions I make at work, etc." Include all of the areas of your life in which you experience anxiety.

....

2. Prayerfully empty yourself of everything that makes you arrogant.

Confess your sins to God. All of them. Die to yourself. You might pray, "Father, please show me where I am depending on myself and not you. Help me depend on you for strength like I depend on air for life." Now, pray specifically about areas where you want to learn to depend on the Holy Spirit. It might help you to pray through the following passages.

> *Truly, truly, I say to you, unless a grain of wheat falls into the earth and dies, it remains alone; but if it dies, it bears much fruit.*
>
> John 12:24

I have been crucified with Christ. It is no longer I who live, but Christ who lives in me. And the life I now live in the flesh I live by faith in the Son of God, who loved me and gave himself for me.

Galatians 2:20

3. Pray for God to fill you with his Holy Spirit.

You might ask, "God, would you help me to drink in the Holy Spirit and keep drinking in the Holy Spirit all day?" Rely upon the Holy Spirit's power to enable you to do what you cannot do by yourself. Ask God to give you faith to believe that you are filled with the Holy Spirit. Ask God to make you responsive to each of his promptings in your life.

4. Give thanks.

We exercise faith when we thank God for what he promised to give us. Now it's time to consciously depend on the Holy Spirit as you walk through your day! Get up. Go walk in the Spirit.

Get Ready for Group

Write your memorized scripture.

_____

_____

_____

_____

_____

What observations and interpretations of scripture were most meaningful to you?

_____

_____

_____

_____

Summarize your key takeaway(s) for this week.

_____

_____

_____

_____

What will you tell the group about the results of your exercise this week?

_____

_____

_____

_____

_____

How has this week helped you better understand and apply the Spiritual Growth Grid?

_____

_____

_____

_____

_____

REPENT & BELIEVE			
WHO GOD IS	**WHAT GOD DID**	**WHO WE ARE**	**WHAT WE DO**
KING	CALLED	CITIZENS	LISTEN & OBEY
FATHER	ADOPTED	FAMILY	LOVE & SERVE
SAVIOR	SENT	MISSIONARIES	GO & MULTIPLY

06

SPIRITUAL DISCIPLINES (PART 1)

SCRIPTURE MEMORY

Have nothing to do with irreverent, silly myths. Rather train yourself for godliness; for while bodily training is of some value, godliness is of value in every way, as it holds promise for the present life and also for the life to come. *–1 Timothy 4:7-8*

WHY DISCIPLINES?

Scripture Study

1 Timothy 4:7-10

Have nothing to do with irreverent, silly myths. Rather train yourself for godliness; [8] for while bodily training is of some value, godliness is of value in every way, as it holds promise for the present life and also for the life to come. [9] The saying is trustworthy and deserving of full acceptance. [10] For to this end we toil and strive, because we have our hope set on the living God, who is the Savior of all people, especially of those who believe.

Observing the Text

What reasons does Paul give for believers to train themselves for godliness?

_____

_____

_____

What other verbs (in addition to train) describe how believers work toward godliness?

_____

_____

Interpreting the Text

In what ways does godliness "hold promise for the present life and also for the life to come"?

_____

_____

_____

What does hope (v. 10) have to do with training for godliness? What is the connection?

_____

_____

_____

In week three, we learned that spiritual growth includes both God's activity and our activity. We are commanded to grow, but we do not have the power to make ourselves grow. Like the farmer, we can cultivate conditions for growth, but only God makes things grow. Like the captain of a sailboat, we can set the sails, but only God brings the wind.

For God's part, he gives us his Holy Spirit — that's why we spent the last two weeks learning about the Holy Spirit and what it means to be filled with him. Our part includes spiritual disciplines. This week and the next will help us understand and apply the basics of spiritual disciplines. Volumes have been written on each of the scores of spiritual disciplines, so we will not be comprehensive. We will focus on the life-giving foundations of spiritual disciplines and the practice known as The Rule of Life.

The principle of duration states, "The *why* determines the *how long*." If we have a really compelling reason to practice a habit, we will continue the habit. If we stop practicing a good habit, it's not because we've forgotten how to do it. Rather, it's likely that we've lost sight of why it's important. So if we want to establish new practices in our lives, the big question that must be answered is, "Why?"

Spiritual disciplines are habits that we practice over a lifetime. Disciplines may be difficult, time-consuming, and demanding. There are many reasons we might quit practicing spiritual disciplines, but the one reason we will stick with the disciplines is that we have a big, compelling why!

As you read today's passage, did you notice the big, compelling reason why we practice spiritual disciplines? Paul illustrates his point with a sports metaphor. We might not all be athletes, but Paul believed that thinking about athletic training helps us best understand how spiritual disciplines work. He says that we can get distracted by lesser things he calls "irreverent, silly myths," or things like video games, Facebook stalking, or binge-watching Netflix. But he urges Timothy and the rest of us to make training a priority.

Most of us would not be able to run a marathon today, no matter how hard we tried. But if we took the time to train, the likelihood that we could finish the grueling 26.2-mile race would increase dramatically. We can do by training what we cannot do by simply trying.

Paul is talking about spiritual training, and using the spiritual disciplines as our training habits. But when it comes to this kind of training, what are we training for? Here's that big, compelling why: godliness. To be godly is to become like God. Godliness is godlikeness, and it doesn't happen all at once. It requires spiritual growth. This process of becoming godly is what the Bible calls sanctification.

Now, let's be clear: we will never be God. But we can train for godliness.

But where do we start? How do we know what godliness looks like? When God wanted us to see what he is like, he showed us Jesus. In Christ, we saw that God is loving, full of peace, patient, forgiving, righteous, holy, and true to his promises. He is gentle, courageous, servant-hearted, submissive and obedient. And all these traits are only a hint at the depth of the beauty of who God is.

God uses spiritual disciplines like the ones discussed in this study to build a god-like character into us. We train ourselves so that our automatic responses to life are more like the automatic responses of Jesus in every circumstance. But it's not a self-help regimen. It's not about us becoming better people, which would make us the central focus of spiritual habits. Rather, spiritual disciplines are all about God, and the result is people who have obviously been changed.

And just like someone who tans because they spend a lot of time in the sun, we are changed by being in the presence of God. But instead of becoming tan, we become godly. We gradually learn to respond to situations in our lives in ways that resemble how Jesus would respond in the same circumstances. In order to experience such a change, we can't just try harder. We must train.

We all know change is not easy. Spiritual disciplines are difficult in the same way that exercise is difficult. Paul says in verse 10, "For to this end we toil and strive, because we have our hope set on the living God." The end is godliness, but extreme diligence is required in becoming godly. He says that we must be so passionate about becoming godly that we are willing to suffer for it. We must go through the toil of training, even when we don't feel like it, and even if it's painful.

However, while training is hard, it's not the hardest way to do something. People sometimes think that doing something like learning to play Bach on the piano by spending years practicing scales and chord progressions is the hard way. Imagine trying as hard as you can to play Bach, without ever having learned a scale or chord progression, or how to read music, or the difference between the white keys and the black keys on a piano. That would be the hard way. The truth is that spending years practicing scales is the best way to learn to play Bach.

This brings us to the relationship of training and actually performing. (I am not saying that we are performing in our spiritual life to earn God's favor. Neither do we perform as if we are actors. Rather, I use the word perform in the same way an athlete seeks to perform his or her best at the moment of the race.)

Here's the key idea: we prepare *off the spot* to perform *on the spot*. Imagine a track coach talking to his runners at the first practice of the year. He wants them to be a championship team, so he teaches them to prepare *off the spot* in order to perform *on the spot*.

The races happen *on the spot*, when each runner lines up against his opponent at a certain time and place. While races are run *on the spot*, every coach will tell his athletes that championships are won *off the spot*, in those moments when no crowd has gathered and no one is looking. People succeed in their performance because they practiced winning in their preparation.

Off the spot, athletes prepare by lifting weights, running drills, practicing starts, running sprints, eating nutritious food (and staying away from junk foods), developing a strong mental game, and going to bed on time. When training gets hard, they remind themselves that championships are not won by trying — they are won by training. The athletes will perform *on the spot the way* they do because of all they did to prepare *off the spot*.

Godly people all have something in common: they have scheduled intentional habits *off the spot* that help them be successful *on the spot*. These disciples have learned to believe the gospel in every aspect of their life through practice and preparation. But what are the spiritual disciplines that are vital to our preparation as disciples? That's what the next lesson is about.

Questions for Reflection

In what ways are you doing more trying than training? How do these look different in a believer's life?

_____

_____

_____

What difference does it make when we see spiritual disciplines as practice and preparation for applying the gospel in every aspect of our lives?

_____

_____

_____

Do you need to repent of using spiritual disciplines as self-help tools rather than opportunities to pursue him as a person? What false beliefs are exposed when we try to achieve godliness on our own?

_____

_____

_____

Prayer

Thank God for sending his son Jesus to show us his perfect character in human flesh. Pray that his Spirit, present within each believer, would grow you in godliness as you passionately pursue him.

SCRIPTURE MEMORY

Have nothing to do with irreverent, silly myths. Rather _____ for godliness; for while bodily training is of some value, _____ is of value in every way, as it holds promise for the present life and also for the _____ _____. *—1 Timothy 4:7-8*

TIME ALONE WITH GOD (PART 1)

Scripture Study

Mark 1:35

And rising very early in the morning, while it was still dark, he [Jesus] departed and went out to a desolate place, and there he prayed.

Observing the Text

When did Jesus get up?

_____

_____

_____

Where did Jesus go?

_____

_____

_____

Interpreting the Text

Why do you think Jesus chose the time and place that he did in this passage?

_____

_____

_____

Why do you think Jesus set apart time to pray?

_____

_____

_____

Teaching

We train to become godly. Spiritual disciplines are training exercises that prepare us to respond to all of life in the way Jesus would respond if he were living in our place. Through spiritual disciplines we walk with God, and exposure to God makes us more like him. Disciplines are difficult sometimes but necessary always.

What are the spiritual disciplines that Christians practice in order to become godly? It's helpful to divide them into two categories: internal and external disciplines. Internal disciplines are reflective habits that require us to go slow and be quiet. External disciplines are communal habits that call for us to be with people, being known and serving one another. We might consider the two categories quiet time and loud time.

Here is a brief list of internal disciplines:

Personal Reading of Scripture

Prayer

Journaling

Meditation

Scripture memorization

Fasting

Solitude

Simplicity

We do these in the quiet. We retreat and slow down to practice these disciplines.

Here is a brief list of external disciplines:

Corporate worship

Small group meetings / Community

Corporate prayer

Confessing sins to one another

Giving

Serving

Witnessing

We do these with others. We open our lives in community to practice these disciplines.

Of course, some of the internal and external disciplines overlap, and all of the disciplines are important, for various reasons. Two of the most significant ways that God helps us grow (marriage and suffering) are not disciplines at all. Next week we're going to discuss the external disciplines, but for the next two lessons we'll be studying the internal disciplines. In this study, we don't have time to address all the disciplines listed above, so we will focus on one fundamental practice.

Jesus modeled the regular practice of the internal disciplines. Although he was busy, he devoted himself to spending time with God the Father. Take a minute to meditate on the following two passages. What do they teach us about time alone with God?

> *And rising very early in the morning, while it was still dark, he departed and went out to a desolate place, and there he prayed.*
>
> Mark 1:35

> *But now even more the report about him went abroad, and great crowds gathered to hear him and to be healed of their infirmities. But he would withdraw to desolate places and pray.*
>
> Luke 5:15-16

Time alone with God was Jesus' priority. He got up early to spend time with his Father. Even if great crowds clamored for his attention and energy, he regularly withdrew from the frenzy. Jesus knew he needed uninterrupted time in a place that was outside the reach of demanding voices and urgent expectations. So he went to a *"desolate"* place, turned off his cell phone, and communed with God.

Do you spend regular time alone with God? We need it, even more than Jesus did. Yet, our need is not enough to make it a regular practice. We need a plan and a place. For most people, it will need to happen early in the morning. For some, it will be late at night. But like Jesus, the only way we get out of the frenzy and into a quiet place is when we do it on purpose. The only way we spend time alone with God on a regular basis is when it becomes a priority.

We must overcome our cultural aversions to being alone, to being quiet, and to slowing down. We are accustomed to noise: music playing in the background, the television blaring, and our cell phones buzzing with notifications. Time alone with God demands that we separate ourselves from the fray to seek God through a number of disciplines such as scripture reading, meditation, journaling, and prayer. Each contributes to a dialogue with God. Everyone develops a unique way of spending time with God, just like couples develop a personal and unique way of communicating with one another. But before we have a unique way of relating to God, let's start with the basics.

Get ready: Have your Bible, a journal, and a pen in the place where you will spend time alone with God. Leave your phone and your computer far from this sacred spot.

Go to bed on time: We win the battle to get up on time by what we do the night before. Set your alarm. Ask God to help you get up and spend time with him. When you get up, move resolutely to the place where you will spend time with God.

Start with the Bible: When we open our Bibles, God opens his mouth. God speaks to us through the scriptures, so part of spending time with God includes scripture reading in some form. We are not reading primarily for information. We are reading to hear God's voice in our lives. We can begin by simply asking God to speak to us before we read. One of the keys to consistency is to have a reading plan.

Meditate on what you read: The word for meditation comes from the idea of a cow chewing its cud. We keep chewing on it — we ruminate — and consider the implications for our lives. We must slow down to meditate. Otherwise, we might be tempted to check off the box and race into the day.

Write your thoughts in a journal: Using a journal helps us think about what God might be saying and how we are to repent and believe. A journal will help us slow down too, but we should limit ourselves to a page (or even a half-page) so that our journaling does not overwhelm our real purpose of communing with God.

Prayer is essential: As a matter of fact, prayer is the seminal internal discipline. It's so important that we will give the entire next lesson to prayer in our time alone with God.

Several years ago, a Chinese pastor spoke to a gathering of Christian leaders about his experience during the Red Revolution in China. As a Christian, he had been put into a concentration camp. Here's some of what he said:

> My friends wonder what kind of work I did when I was in the labor camp that kept me healthy and sane. I answer them that life in the labor camp is very, very hard. The authorities in the camp put me to emptying the human waste cesspool. Most of the prisoners were afraid to approach the cesspool, but the authorities were aware of my background. I was well educated, from a well-to-do family. And especially because they were atheists and I was a Christian leader, they put me there. They enjoyed putting me to work in a human waste cesspool. But they did not know through the years how much I enjoyed working there.

> The cesspool was two meters in breadth, two meters in length filled with human waste collected from the entire camp. Once it was full, the human waste was kept until it was ripe, and then it was dug out and sent to the fields as fertilizer. Because the pit was so deep, I could not reach the bottom to empty it. So I had to walk into the disease-ridden mass and scoop out the successive layers of waste, all the time being forced to breathe the stench. The guards and the other prisoners kept a long way off because of the stench.

> So why did I enjoy working in the cesspool? I enjoyed the

solitude. In the labor camp all the prisoners were under strict surveillance, and no one could be left alone. But when I worked in the cesspool, I could be alone and I could pray to the Lord daily as loudly as I needed. I could recite scripture, including all the Psalms that I had ever memorized. And no one would protest. That's the reason I enjoyed working the cesspool. And I could sing loudly the hymns that I remembered. In those days, one of my favorite Christian hymns was, "In the Garden." Before I was arrested it was my favorite hymn, but before I was arrested I did not understand the real meaning of the hymn. When I worked in the cesspool, I discovered a wonderful fellowship with the Lord. Again and again, I sang this hymn, and I felt the Lord's presence with me:

I come to the garden alone, while the dew is still on the roses
And the voice I hear falling on my ear, the Son of God discloses
And he walks with me and he talks with me and he tells me I am his own
And the joy we share as we tarry there, none other has ever known.

As I sang this hymn in the cesspool, I experienced the Lord's presence. He never left me, nor did he forsake me.[1]

There is a secret place where we meet with God. Elijah, through the frenzy of earthquakes and wildfires, was taken to a cave where he heard God's still, small voice. Moses met with God on Mount Sinai, and then later in the Tent of Meeting outside the camp. John the Baptist chose to live in the wilderness. Jesus taught us to go into a closet and modeled going to a desolate place. Peter went up on the roof to pray and be alone with God,

---

[1] Heard in a sermon at Willow Creek Community Church by John Ortberg.

and God led him to do something that had never been done before: taking the gospel to the Gentiles, which opened the door for the whole world to experience intimacy and communion with God.

How, where, and when will you spend time alone with God?

Questions for Reflection

Is it difficult for you to slow down and get quiet? What do you need to change to make this internal discipline a priority?

_____

_____

_____

When will you devote yourself to spend time alone with God? Where will you meet with him? What is your plan?

_____

_____

_____

You may have previously approached this discipline as a duty or requirement, something that "good" Christians do, rather than an opportunity to spend time with your Father. What does this mindset reveal about our beliefs about God's character and how our sanctification is accomplished?

_____

_____

_____

What would change if you repented of this way of thinking by approaching time alone with God as a privilege?

_____

_____

_____

Prayer

Praise our God who desires intimacy with his children, who made a way through the blood of his Son for us to meet with him, hear his voice, and know his love. Ask him to give you a deep desire for time alone with him.

SCRIPTURE MEMORY

Have nothing to do with irreverent,

_____. Rather train yourself for

_____; for while _____

is of some value, godliness is of value

in every way, as it _____ for

the present life and also for the life to

come. *—1 Timothy 4:7-8*

TIME ALONE WITH GOD (PART 2)

Scripture Study

Luke 11:1-4

Now Jesus was praying in a certain place, and when he finished, one of his disciples said to him, "Lord, teach us to pray, as John taught his disciples."
2 And he said to them, "When you pray, say:
"Father, hallowed be your name.
Your kingdom come.
3 Give us each day our daily bread,
4 and forgive us our sins,
for we ourselves forgive everyone who is indebted to us.
And lead us not into temptation."

Matthew 6:9-15

Pray then like this:
"Our Father in heaven,
hallowed be your name.
10 Your kingdom come,
your will be done,

on earth as it is in heaven.

[11] Give us this day our daily bread,

[12] and forgive us our debts,

as we also have forgiven our debtors.

[13] And lead us not into temptation,

but deliver us from evil.

[14] For if you forgive others their trespasses, your heavenly Father will also forgive you, [15] but if you do not forgive others their trespasses, neither will your Father forgive your trespasses.

Observing the Text

What did the disciple ask to learn? (Luke 11:1)

_____

_____

_____

What differences do you see between these two passages?

_____

_____

_____

Interpreting the Text

Why does it matter that the passages aren't identical?

_____

_____

_____

What do these passages teach us about how to pray?

_____

_____

_____

Teaching

Jesus' disciples had seen a lot of people pray. But when Jesus prayed, something was different. It worked. So they asked Jesus to teach them to pray. Who taught you how to brush your teeth or throw a ball? Even the most basic skills of life must be taught, and prayer is no different. We learn to pray by listening to others pray, and we get comfortable praying by praying. It's like learning to swim: we can talk about it all we want, but we only learn to swim by getting in the water. We can learn about prayer from what Jesus said, but eventually we must get in the water.

Look back at the Scripture passages you studied this week. Jesus taught his disciples to pray at their request. The disciples did not ask Jesus to teach them a prayer. They asked him to teach them how to pray. Notice the two versions of the model prayer are not verbatim, which indicates this is not a prayer to recite. Actually, Jesus taught his disciples in Matthew 6:7 to not pray with vain repetition, saying words that do not require our heart or our mental-emotional engagement. Jesus' model prayer is not repeated a single time by any Christ-follower in the New Testament. Instead, we use it as a guide to follow.

In response to his disciples, Jesus gave seven topics of prayer. As we survey each topic, we will look at how Jesus' model teaches us to pray.

Father: We address God as Father. He adopted us into his family through Christ. In prayer, we acknowledge that he loves us and is inclined to answer our requests. As we accept how God feels about us, we will be motivated to talk to God with confidence.

Example: Father, thank you for loving me and watching over me. I believe you love me more than I love my kids. You are a good, good Father.

Hallowed be your name: As we begin to pray, we do not just read off a list of what we want from God. We praise God. *Hallowed* means holy. In biblical times, a name was not simply a designation to keep people from being confused with someone else in the way that we use names. Rather, a name was a designation of character, authority, and essence. God's name shows us who he is and what he has committed to do for us. When we begin our prayers with praise, we see the world correctly and ourselves more accurately. God is holy. We need him. He is all-powerful and all-knowing. We are not. Praise gives us hope and compels us to appeal to no other source for our needs than the loving heavenly Father who is both willing and able to answer our prayers.

Example: Father in Heaven, you created all things. You bring order to the chaos. You made me, so you know exactly what I need.

Your kingdom come: The kingdom of God is not a geographical kingdom (John 18:36). Rather, when Jesus refers to the kingdom, he's talking about the reign or control of God. Jesus is reigning in heaven and, by invitation, in the hearts of his people. As we saw in the beginning of this study, our natural response to the coming of the kingdom is to repent and believe the good news (Mark 1:15). So Jesus teaches us to regularly surrender our kingdoms and our will to God's kingdom and will.

Example: Father, I want your will about whether I take this new job. I surrender my desire to control the outcomes. I ask that you would direct the minds of those who are making the decision and shape my desires in accordance with your plan. I pray that my work will be more about you and your kingdom than me and my wants.

Give us each day our daily bread: Twenty times in the New Testament, God tells us to ask him for things we need. He wants us to ask for everything we need, even the food we will eat each day. When we ask for our most basic needs, we are reminded that God provides everything. To think otherwise is prideful and ungrateful. On the other hand, when we ask God for our most basic needs, even though our pantry is full and our closets have plenty, we are acknowledging that he is our source. We need him, and we need him to provide for us.

Example: Father, I ask you to continue to provide new clients, grant me favor with my customers, and help me to serve them well. I pray you would give our family energy for the day, health, food, the money we need, and wisdom. We trust you alone to be our provider.

Forgive us our sins: There is a difference between sins and sin. Sins are acts of rebellion against God, but sin is the prideful condition of one's heart that insists on one's own way. God dealt with our sin at the cross where our spiritual debt was paid—past, present, and future. Yet we still commit sins against God. And while our sins don't place followers of Jesus under judgment, our sins wound us and others, grieving the Holy Spirit and making us feel distant from God. Confessing our sins fights these damaging effects. To *confess* means "to say the same thing." When we confess our sins, we say the same thing that God does about our sins, without defense or excuse. In response to our confession, God cleanses and heals us, helping us to feel closer to him. So even though God forgave our sin when we placed our faith in Jesus, we take time in prayer to confess our sins.

Example: Father, please forgive me for my outburst of anger toward Debbie. I need you to fill me with your Holy Spirit so I can respond to disappointments in a way that honors you.

As we forgive everyone indebted to us: Forgiveness of others is a family trait in God's family, and Jesus urges us to take time to choose forgiveness in prayer. Forgiveness is a choice followed by a process. In other words, we choose to forgive someone before we feel like we have forgiven them.

After we make the choice, God works in our hearts over time to help us release our desire to punish or hurt that person. In prayer, we bring before God the people who have offended us, and we forgive them. We ask for his help to love them, even if they are our enemies.

Example: Father, I want to forgive James. What he did was wrong. I confess that I want to make him pay. But you forgave me when I was wrong. You did not make me pay. So, with your help, I will put away my hate. I will not keep my hurt alive by telling this story to others. It stops here, with you.

And lead us not into temptation: We have a powerful, personal enemy who seeks our destruction (1 Peter 5:8). Because Satan's attacks are real, Jesus taught us to pray for God's help in the midst of a world fraught with temptation. In prayer, we can tune our hearts and minds to see the schemes of the devil and avoid sinful traps that the enemy sets to deceive us. We can pray for God's help to overcome specific, habitual sins.

Example: Father, please protect me from temptations to try to flatter people or impress people as I attend the conference today. Give me eyes to see any traps set by the enemy, because I know that I am susceptible to selfishness and self-promotion. Grant me humility and a heart of service.

Is it necessary for us to follow this outline each time we pray? No. You can simply talk to God from the heart, anytime and anywhere. But Jesus' model prayer is given as a guide for prayer so we can know the matters about which we must pray. If we exclude one of the topics that Jesus taught us to pray about, we must include that topic in our prayers in the future.

As we learn to spend time with God, we will discover a new kind of satisfaction. It's the kind of satisfaction that C.S. Lewis depicts in *The Chronicles of Narnia* when a girl named Jill meets Aslan, the massive lion who is the Lord of Narnia (and the symbolic figure of Christ).

"Are you not thirsty?" said the Lion.

"I am dying of thirst," said Jill.

"Then drink," said the Lion.

"May I—could I—would you mind going away while I do?" said Jill.

The Lion answered this only by a look and a very low growl. And as Jill gazed at its motionless bulk, she realized that she might as well have asked the whole mountain to move aside for her convenience.

The delicious rippling noise of the stream was driving her nearly frantic. "Will you promise not to—do anything to me, if I do come?" said Jill.

"I make no promise," said the Lion.

Jill was so thirsty now that, without noticing it, she had come a step nearer. "Do you eat girls?" she said.

"I have swallowed up girls and boys, women and men, kings and emperors, cities and realms," said the Lion. It didn't say this as if it were boasting, nor as if it were sorry, nor as if it were angry. It just said it.

"I dare not come and drink," said Jill.

"Then you will die of thirst," said the Lion.

"Oh dear!" said Jill, coming another step nearer. "I suppose I must go and look for another stream then."

"There is no other stream," said the Lion. [1]

People dying of thirst are constantly searching, but there is no other stream. As we consider the pathway of spiritual formation and the inclusion of internal disciplines, it's important to remember that we are people who are learning to drink from the one and only stream that will satisfy our souls.

---

1 C. S. Lewis, *The Silver Chair* (New York: HarperCollins, 1953), 16-17.

Questions for Reflection

Where did you learn how to pray? How did that teaching differ from what Jesus showed his disciples in the model prayer?

_____

_____

_____

Which of the topics in the model prayer are you most likely to minimize or forget? What does that reveal about your beliefs regarding God's character?

_____

_____

_____

In what streams are you seeking satisfaction? Take time to repent of pursuing lesser sources of joy while neglecting the living fountain.

_____

_____

_____

What do you need to believe more deeply about God in order to place your hope solely in him?

_____

_____

_____

Prayer

Thank God for being a good Father who is willing to listen when we pray and gives us all we need. Pray that he would deliver us from the temptation to trust ourselves so that we would instead turn to him in dependent prayer.

WEEKLY EXERCISE

FOLLOWING OUR MODEL

In your time alone with God this week, practice praying through the model prayer, topic by topic. Remember this is not a formula, but rather a guideline to remind us of the various ways in which we relate to our Father. He deserves our praise and submission. He provides for our needs and forgives our sins. He strengthens us when we struggle to forgive and obey. May our prayers reflect the depth of his goodness as we walk with him daily in the light of his grace.

Our Father: Begin by praying in a way that proclaims God's love for you and your place in his family, with a heart of gratitude and joy.

....

Hallowed be your name: Praise God in specific ways that highlight his absolute uniqueness, declaring his creativity, beauty, power, and worth.

....

Your kingdom come: Invite God to reign in your life and heart today, surrendering all things to his lordship and submitting your will to his.

....

Give us this day our daily bread: Acknowledge that God is the source of provision for all your needs, humbly asking that he would faithfully give you the resources to serve him well today.

....

Forgive us our sins: Confess the ways that you have failed to display Christ's character today, agreeing with God about your sins without excuse or blame. Then, give thanks that God has promised to forgive and restore those who confess their sins to him.

As we forgive everyone indebted to us: Ask God to help you choose forgiveness in response to hurt, releasing your desire to punish the offender and extending his love in spite of their action.

....

And lead us not into temptation: Examine yourself for specific, habitual temptations with which Satan is attacking you, pleading with God for the Spirit's power to stand up under them.

Get Ready for Group

Write your memorized scripture.

_____

_____

_____

_____

_____

What observations and interpretations of scripture were most meaningful to you?

_____

_____

_____

_____

_____

Summarize your key takeaway(s) for this week.

_____

_____

_____

_____

_____

What will you tell the group about the results of your exercise this week?

_____

_____

_____

_____

_____

How has this week helped you better understand and apply the Spiritual Growth Grid?

_____

_____

_____

_____

_____

	REPENT & BELIEVE		
WHO GOD IS	WHAT GOD DID	WHO WE ARE	WHAT WE DO
KING	CALLED	CITIZENS	LISTEN & OBEY
FATHER	ADOPTED	FAMILY	LOVE & SERVE
SAVIOR	SENT	MISSIONARIES	GO & MULTIPLY

07

SPIRITUAL DISCIPLINES (PART 2)

SCRIPTURE MEMORY

Have nothing to do with irreverent, silly myths. Rather train yourself for godliness; for while bodily training is of some value, godliness is of value in every way, as it holds promise for the present life and also for the life to come. *−1 Timothy 4:7-8*

EXTERNAL DISCIPLINES

Scripture Study

Hebrews 10:19-25

Therefore, brothers, since we have confidence to enter the holy places by the blood of Jesus, [20] *by the new and living way that he opened for us through the curtain, that is, through his flesh,* [21] *and since we have a great priest over the house of God,* [22] *let us draw near with a true heart in full assurance of faith, with our hearts sprinkled clean from an evil conscience and our bodies washed with pure water.* [23] *Let us hold fast the confession of our hope without wavering, for he who promised is faithful.* [24] *And let us consider how to stir up one another to love and good works,* [25] *not neglecting to meet together, as is the habit of some, but encouraging one another, and all the more as you see the Day drawing near.*

Observing the Text

Circle any words in the passage that imply "community." What did this community have in common? (See verses 19-21.)

_____

_____

_____

Based on what the recipients of this letter had in common, what does the writer of this passage encourage people to do together?

_____

_____

_____

Interpreting the Text

What is the source of our confidence (v. 19) as followers of Jesus?

_____

_____

_____

In what ways is the gospel both individual and communal? Which aspect is being emphasized in this passage? Why do you think that is?

_____

_____

_____

Teaching

Our part in spiritual growth includes practicing both internal and external spiritual disciplines. While this study will not consider all of the spiritual disciplines, we will consider the most basic ones. Today, we'll focus on external spiritual disciplines.

Remember, the external disciplines include:

Corporate worship

Small group meetings / Community

Corporate prayer

Confessing sins to one another

Giving

Serving

Witnessing

We do these with others. Each of these disciplines requires that we open our lives to other people, to know and be known. The most fundamental of these external disciplines is community.

What do people in a Christian community have in common? What makes us "brothers"? The answer is described in Hebrews 10:19-21. We believe Jesus made it possible for us to come before a holy God when he shed his blood on the cross to pay for our sins. Furthermore, Jesus is not only the sacrifice for our sins that brought us forgiveness, but he is the "great priest over the house of God" who mediates between us and a holy God so that we have confidence to come to God in "full assurance of faith."

Simply stated, we believe the gospel. Therefore, our faith in Jesus and his work on our behalf gives us a unique connection with one another and with God. This unique connection includes responsibilities to one another.

The writer of Hebrews directs his readers to live out their faith together, highlighting three of the many responsibilities of Christian community. These three responsibilities are a good place to start.

We Believe Together

> *Let us hold fast the confession of our hope without wavering, for he who promised is faithful.*
>
> Hebrews 10:23

Believing is not an individual exercise. It's a community responsibility.

We might think that our belief is simply a matter of personal choice, but beliefs take root in a community.

As I (Bruce) was growing in my faith, I made a negative comment about myself to a mentor. As a mature Christian, he was able to discern that the beliefs behind my statement were filled with wrong thinking. He responded by asking me, "Who told you that?" When I reacted with confusion, he continued, "Someone told you that, but it's not true. If you know where that belief came from, it will be easier for you to correct it." His assumption was that we do not come to our beliefs alone. The writer of Hebrews agrees.

I was in a small group when a group member struggling with doubt asked for prayer about some specific challenges in his family. He then wondered if the prayers would even matter since he had doubts. Another group member responded, "Even if you struggle to believe, you need to know that we believe, so we will pray." The group was holding fast to the confession of our hope, even though this group member was struggling to believe himself.

Often, faith is borrowed before it's owned. But some fail to *hold fast the confession of our hope* because they have neglected the first two words: "Let us." They are trying to do it alone. Our beliefs grow deeper when we believe together.

We Grow Together

And let us consider how to stir up one another to love and good works.

Hebrews 10:24

When we believe together, we also grow together. Often, the greatest times of growth in life are associated with other people who inspire and encourage us. For years, my wife and I were part of a gym. Three days a week, before the sun broke over the horizon, we worked out with a few other people. We pushed and stretched ourselves farther than ever before. What was the difference between working out alone and working out with a group? We were part of a little community committed to growing together. We would "stir up one another" to greater intensity in workouts. Thus, we were in the shape of our lives.

Something similar happens when we are around people who have an intense commitment to follow Jesus. In community, there is insight, inspiration, and there are people to imitate. In community, we are stirred up to serve, to forgive, to be generous, and to risk following Jesus in ways we haven't followed before. That's growing together.

We Endure Together

Not neglecting to meet together, as is the habit of some, but encouraging one another, and all the more as you see the Day drawing near.

Hebrews 10:25

Why do people who were once faithful followers of Jesus fall away? Undoubtedly, there are many reasons. But one of the most common causes is that people tried to go it alone. We endure better together. When we discipline ourselves to stay engaged in community, we encourage each other to press on, even when things get hard.

When you run a race, having someone to cheer you on helps to keep you from giving up. That's the picture here. He is talking about the finish line, the day when our race in this life is done, the day when Jesus Christ comes again for his people. If you run this difficult race alone, chances are good that you will not finish. The word translated *encouraging* literally means "to come alongside." There is a phrase often cited as an African proverb that sums up this idea of community well, "If you want to go fast, go alone. If you want to go far, go together." That's how community works. We need people alongside us to help us finish.

Questions for Reflection

How have you experienced the benefits and responsibilities of participation in Christian community?

_____

_____

_____

How is participating in Christian community at times a countercultural choice?

_____

_____

_____

What false beliefs about our identity are revealed when we avoid Christian community?

_____

_____

_____

What does it demonstrate about God's character that he desires us to not only be in community with him but also with each other?

_____

_____

_____

Prayer

Thank God for surrounding you with other believers who are pursuing belief, growth, and endurance together. Pray that he would give you the courage and faithfulness to know and be known, love and be loved, serve and be served.

SCRIPTURE MEMORY

Have _____,

_____. Rather train yourself for

godliness; for while bodily training

is of some value, _____

_____, as it holds promise

for the present life and also for the

life to come. *–1 Timothy 4:7-8*

DEVELOPING CHRISTIAN COMMUNITY

Scripture Study

Hebrews 10:19-25

Therefore, brothers, since we have confidence to enter the holy places by the blood of Jesus, ²⁰ by the new and living way that he opened for us through the curtain, that is, through his flesh, ²¹ and since we have a great priest over the house of God, ²² let us draw near with a true heart in full assurance of faith, with our hearts sprinkled clean from an evil conscience and our bodies washed with pure water. ²³ Let us hold fast the confession of our hope without wavering, for he who promised is faithful. ²⁴ And let us consider how to stir up one another to love and good works, ²⁵ not neglecting to meet together, as is the habit of some, but encouraging one another, and all the more as you see the Day drawing near.

Observing the Text

Circle all the words or phrases above that you recognize as connections to the Old Testament Law. Try to think of the original readers' context.

_____

_____

What actions does the author call for believers to do in these verses? List the specific verbs.

_____

_____

_____

Interpreting the Text

How does this passage describe Jesus' fulfillment of the Law? What benefits do believers gain from this?

_____

_____

_____

How does the author connect our actions in community with God's character?

_____

_____

_____

Teaching

People experience community around shared values. That's why there are book clubs, internet forums, and fantasy football leagues. But you don't have to share multiple common interests to experience Christian community with people. Rather, Christians have a unique opportunity for community because we share our deepest value and highest treasure, Jesus Christ. We can experience Christian community when we connect with others who worship and follow Jesus. But we must do more than simply attend church services together to develop community.

When people gather for church services, the level of connection is not deep enough to facilitate the responsibilities of Christian community we see in Hebrews 10:19-25. We have to connect more deeply and more personally. We need to move from sitting in rows (as we do in worship services) to sitting in circles (as we do in small groups).

Small groups are one strategy for developing Christian community. We hope that everyone who attends a small group experiences the wonderful benefits and joys of Christian community, but they might not. It takes time to develop community, and it takes more than just time to deepen community.

Groups experience varying degrees of community. While some remain shallow and pleasant, others grow closer, deeper, and stronger. What's the difference? What moves a small group from snacks and small talk with a little bit of the Bible mixed in to a Biblical community of maturing disciples in Jesus?

Here are some keys to develop and deepen community:

Have Faith

We must believe what God says about community. The church is the body of Christ (Romans 12:4-5). He is in the midst of his people (Luke 17:20-21). Where two, or more, are gathered in his name, he is with us (Matthew 18:20). We believe together, grow together, and endure together. And if we believe that Christian community is a vital part of worshiping and following Jesus, we will rearrange our lives in order to experience it.

Keep Showing Up

Community requires time. The number one reason people give for not being in a small group is the same reason given for not exercising: they don't have time. When someone does determine to make time for small group, they sometimes have expectations that they are going to "get something out of it" every time they show up. But like exercise, the only way you get something out of it is when you make time for it and keep showing up. And yet just showing up regularly is just the beginning.

Take Risks

Relationships include risks. Committing to show up at someone's house feels like a risk. Getting together with new people, answering questions about what you think, and telling people what you believe are all risks. Disagreeing with someone is a risk. Sharing a prayer request is a risk. Praying out loud with others for the first time feels like a risk. There are risks in every relationship where there is love, respect, mutuality, and service. But these risks have rewards. Over time, trust deepens and opens the door to the biggest risk.

Be Known

All people want to be fully known and fully loved. We want people to know our names, our stories, our hopes, our thoughts, our feelings – our innermost selves. But because we have been hurt before, some of us are not transparent enough to be known. Like Adam and Eve, we cover up our nakedness with fig leaves of image management. Thus, we don't feel loved, because we have to be known to feel loved. Otherwise, when someone shows love toward us, we might think, "But if you really knew me, you wouldn't love me." Developing and deepening Christian community includes the process of becoming known over time. Ultimately, when you are known and loved, you become the person God intended you to be all along. We tend to take this process of being known very slowly, until a catalyst accelerates the process.

Run to the Train Wreck

A train wreck might be suffering, marital stress, a health crisis, a wayward teenager, or any number of other things. When a train wreck comes in a small group, it often helps the group get honest. But in the midst of struggle, the sense of community in the group grows deeper, faster. We might say that groups just *meet together* until the first train wreck in someone's life, then they *come together* to experience real community. We are more likely to stop managing our image. Everyone gets real. The key seems to be that when the train wreck comes, the people in the group run to the train wreck. They don't avoid it or throw platitudes at those suffering, because they know, love, and serve one another.

Gospel First

In Christian community, instead of giving one another good advice in the midst of a struggle or personal challenge, we bring the gospel first. The first step to bring the gospel is reminding one another of how God longs to meet us in our sin and suffering with mercy and grace. So we turn to God in prayer as a group. We seek his wisdom in scripture. We remind each other of promises from God.

Serve One Another

When we experience Christian community in a small group, we grow in our ability to serve one another. In community, it's not all about us. At times, our sole purpose is to serve one another. According to Hebrews 10:19-25, we continue meeting together so that we can stimulate each another to love and good works and encourage one another. When our group demonstrates the commitment to truly serve one another in a way that we are all growing closer, deeper, and stronger in our love for God and others, we get to experience the rare and beautiful gift of community in the way God intended it.

My prayer for you is that you experience the kind of Christian community described above. As community deepens and ages, it becomes one of the greatest gifts we receive in this life. While it's a gift from God, we contribute to the development of this community too by the way we treat one another.

Questions for Reflection

In what ways is it countercultural to seek community with people who aren't just like you in all the ways people can see?

_____

_____

_____

What difference can it make when we truly believe that each follower of Jesus is a beloved member of God's family?

_____

_____

_____

Which of the keys to developing and deepening community is most difficult for you? Why?

_____

_____

_____

Which have you seen make the biggest difference in your group experiences? How?

_____

_____

_____

Prayer

Thank God for the gift of Christian community — that we don't have to do this life alone but instead are part of a body with other believers. Ask that he would give you both the courage to be fully known and the compassion to love and serve the other members of your group.

SCRIPTURE MEMORY

_____ irreverent,

silly myths. _____

_____; for while bodily training

is of some value, _____

_____, as it holds promise for

_____ and also _____

_____. –_1 Timothy 4:7-8_

THE DANGER OF SPIRITUAL DISCIPLINES

Scripture Study

Galatians 3:1-11

O foolish Galatians! Who has bewitched you? It was before your eyes that Jesus Christ was publicly portrayed as crucified. ² Let me ask you only this: Did you receive the Spirit by works of the law or by hearing with faith? 3 Are you so foolish? Having begun by the Spirit, are you now being perfected by the flesh? ⁴ Did you suffer so many things in vain — if indeed it was in vain? ⁵ Does he who supplies the Spirit to you and works miracles among you do so by works of the law, or by hearing with faith — ⁶ just as Abraham "believed God, and it was counted to him as righteousness"?

⁷ Know then that it is those of faith who are the sons of Abraham. ⁸ And the Scripture, foreseeing that God would justify the Gentiles by faith, preached the gospel beforehand to Abraham, saying, "In you shall all the nations be blessed." ⁹ So then, those who are of faith are blessed along with Abraham, the man of faith.

¹⁰ For all who rely on works of the law are under a curse; for it is written,

"Cursed be everyone who does not abide by all things written in the Book of the Law, and do them." [11] *Now it is evident that no one is justified before God by the law, for "The righteous shall live by faith."*

Observing the Text

Paul asks a series of rhetorical questions in verses 2-5. What answers are implied?

_____

_____

_____

In this passage, who does Paul say is blessed? Who does he describe as cursed?

_____

_____

_____

Interpreting the Text

What connection does Paul make between how we began the Christian life and how we continue in it? Why does this matter?

_____

_____

_____

What are the Galatians relying on in this passage? What kinds of things do Christians today tend to rely on to try to earn God's favor?

_____

_____

_____

Teaching

In management circles, leaders talk about the difference between *lead measures* and *lag measures*. Lead measures are the things we have control over. They track what we do regularly that we hope will produce results. Lag measures are the results. For example, a sales team might keep a record of the number of calls each salesperson makes in a certain period of time. That's a lead measure, because salespeople can control the calls they make. But the amount of product sold is a lag measure. A salesperson has less control over the amount of product sold than the calls made.

Spiritual disciplines are like lead measures. We can control how often we practice the disciplines of time alone with God or gathering with people in our small group to experience Christian community. We hope to experience the lag measures of communion with God and the development of godly character traits like love, joy, and peace. But while spiritual disciplines are important lead measures, there are inherent dangers with them.

A friend of mine once commended the spiritual maturity of a man he knew by saying that this man had not missed his daily time alone with God in the last 15 years. That sounds like he had mastered the lead measure of spiritual disciplines. But inside, I groaned. When one's focus is the discipline instead of communion with God, we might be tempted to think more highly of ourselves. In doing the disciplines faithfully, it can be easy to start finding our righteousness in what we do.

We must be careful not to let spiritual disciplines become a new law that we keep to earn God's favor.

Here are some danger signs that we might be trusting in our spiritual disciplines more than the gospel.

- We feel better about ourselves because we have remained faithful to certain spiritual disciplines (or more critical of others who are less disciplined).
- We think God will answer our prayers or give us favor because of our regular disciplines.
- We tell others about our faithfulness in the disciplines because we believe it makes us appear more godly to them.

It may sound like we can't win either way. If we are faithful to practice spiritual disciplines, we might become self-righteous. If we don't practice the disciplines, we will not do our part in spiritual formation. So how do we practice spiritual disciplines without succumbing to the danger of self-righteousness?

Let's go back to the Spiritual Growth Grid, which emphasizes identity before activity. We embrace our new identity based on what Christ has already done for us to make us citizens in his kingdom, children in his family, and missionaries in his plan of redemption. Once we begin to believe who God says we are, spiritual disciplines move from being our requirement to our response. Remember that disciplines require effort, but they are not about earning favor with God. God will not love us more because we read our Bible more often. We read our Bible to connect with God, remind ourselves of his character, and better equip ourselves to do his work.

With a better understanding of our part in spiritual formation, we can develop a strategic plan to repent and believe that utilizes spiritual disciplines as means to know God more, and become more like him.

Questions for Reflection

When have you been guilty of prioritizing spiritual disciplines themselves over communion with God? Review the list of danger signs.

_____

_____

_____

How can an accurate view of our identity in Christ affect our attitude toward the disciplines? What does this look like?

_____

_____

_____

Do you need to repent of a wrong attitude toward the disciplines – either treating them as measures of spirituality that earn us the favor of God and others, or neglecting the importance of their usefulness for our growth in godliness?

_____

_____

_____

What do you need to believe more deeply today about who God is and what he has called you to?

_____

_____

_____

Prayer

Praise the Father for his desire to know us each intimately and for us to know him. Pray that he would deliver us from the temptation to rely on the disciplines to somehow earn our own righteousness, and ask him to empower you to faithfully pursue him above all else.

WEEKLY EXERCISE

A RULE OF LIFE

A Rule of Life[1] is a personal, strategic plan that you design to help you keep God at the center of everything you do. The word "rule" comes from the Greek word for trellis. A trellis is a tool that enables a grapevine to get off the ground and grow upward, becoming more fruitful. So our Rule of Life is a trellis, but we depend on God to bring the growth. The goal with this strategic plan is to live in such a way that we prefer the love of Christ above all things. A Rule of Life is personal and fluid. One must determine by trial and error which disciplines are most helpful in each season of life.

Twelve Elements for a Rule of Life[2]

Prayer
1. Scripture
2. Silence and Solitude
3. Daily Office (Prayer)
4. Study

Rest
5. Sabbath
6. Simplicity / Giving
7. Play and Recreation

Work/Activity
8. Service and Mission
9. Care for the Physical Body

Relationships
10. Emotional Health
11. Family
12. Community

---

1 These thoughts on developing a Rule of Life come from Peter Scazzero, *Emotionally Healthy Spirituality* (Grand Rapids, MI: Zondervan, 2006), 196-198.
2 Ibid., 199-200.

Similarly, Bill Hull refers to 14 spiritual disciplines: Bible reading, meditation, Scripture memorization, prayer, worship, evangelism, service, stewardship, fasting, silence, solitude, journaling, submission, and frugality.[3]

Prayerfully prepare a Rule of Life by writing a strategic plan of the spiritual disciplines that will help you prefer the love of Christ over all things. Identify the discipline and when you will practice it. Begin with what time you will go to bed.[4] Be ready to share your plan with your group so that you can hold each other accountable to pursuing spiritual growth.

---

3 Bill Hull, The Complete Book of Discipleship (Colorado Springs, CO: NavPress, 2006), 193.
4 When one goes to bed is the trigger for disciplines. Keep the rule for bedtime, and you will have an advantage in keeping the other rules you are making for your life.

Get Ready for Group

Write your memorized scripture.

_____

_____

_____

_____

_____

What observations and interpretations of scripture were most meaningful to you?

_____

_____

_____

_____

_____

Summarize your key takeaway(s) for this week.

_____

_____

_____

_____

_____

What will you tell the group about the results of your exercise this week?

_____

_____

_____

_____

_____

How has this week helped you better understand and apply the Spiritual Growth Grid?

_____

_____

_____

_____

_____

REPENT & BELIEVE

WHO GOD IS	WHAT GOD DID	WHO WE ARE	WHAT WE DO
KING	CALLED	CITIZENS	LISTEN & OBEY
FATHER	ADOPTED	FAMILY	LOVE & SERVE
SAVIOR	SENT	MISSIONARIES	GO & MULTIPLY

08

WALKING IN GOD'S POWER

SCRIPTURE MEMORY

But you will receive power when the
Holy Spirit has come upon you, and
you will be my witnesses in Jerusalem and in all Judea and Samaria,
and to the end of the earth. *—Acts 1:8*

ALL OF LIFE IS REPENTANCE

Scripture Study

Luke 3:1-18

In the fifteenth year of the reign of Tiberius Caesar, Pontius Pilate being governor of Judea, and Herod being tetrarch of Galilee, and his brother Philip tetrarch of the region of Ituraea and Trachonitis, and Lysanias tetrarch of Abilene, ² during the high priesthood of Annas and Caiaphas, the word of God came to John the son of Zechariah in the wilderness. ³ And he went into all the region around the Jordan, proclaiming a baptism of repentance for the forgiveness of sins. ⁴ As it is written in the book of the words of Isaiah the prophet,

> *"The voice of one crying in the wilderness:*
> *'Prepare the way of the Lord,*
> *make his paths straight.*
> *⁵ Every valley shall be filled,*
> *and every mountain and hill shall be made low,*
> *and the crooked shall become straight,*
> *and the rough places shall become level ways,*

⁶ and all flesh shall see the salvation of God.'"

⁷ He said therefore to the crowds that came out to be baptized by him, "You brood of vipers! Who warned you to flee from the wrath to come? ⁸ bear fruits in keeping with repentance. And do not begin to say to yourselves, 'We have Abraham as our father.' For I tell you, God is able from these stones to raise up children for Abraham. ⁹ Even now the axe is laid to the root of the trees. Every tree therefore that does not bear good fruit is cut down and thrown into the fire."

¹⁰ And the crowds asked him, "What then shall we do?" ¹¹ And he answered them, "Whoever has two tunics is to share with him who has none, and whoever has food is to do likewise." ¹² Tax collectors also came to be baptized and said to him, "Teacher, what shall we do?" ¹³ And he said to them, "Collect no more than you are authorized to do." ¹⁴ Soldiers also asked him, "And we, what shall we do?" And he said to them, "Do not extort money from anyone by threats or by false accusation, and be content with your wages."

¹⁵ As the people were in expectation, and all were questioning in their hearts concerning John, whether he might be the Christ, ¹⁶ John answered them all, saying, "I baptize you with water, but he who is mightier than I is coming, the strap of whose sandals I am not worthy to untie. He will baptize you with the Holy Spirit and fire. ¹⁷ His winnowing fork is in his hand, to clear his threshing floor and to gather the wheat into his barn, but the chaff he will burn with unquenchable fire." ¹⁸ So with many other exhortations he preached good news to the people.

Observing the Text (v. 1-6)

Who is the main character in this passage? Where does he go and what does he do? (Make sure to focus on just the first six verses; we'll study the remainder of the passage throughout the week.)

_____

_____

_____

In the quotation from Isaiah, what are the tasks that will "prepare the way of the Lord"?

_____

_____

_____

Interpreting the Text

What message is John proclaiming (v. 3)?

_____

_____

_____

How does this message connect to the quotation from Isaiah?

_____

_____

_____

Teaching

The Gospel writer, Luke, reminds us that the Old Testament prophet Isaiah said that someone would come declaring a message from the wilderness for people to prepare the way of the Lord. In Luke 3:1-18, we see those words fulfilled as God used John the Baptist to prepare the world for the coming of Jesus.

Preparing the way of the Lord is a reference to how people prepared the roadway for the king who would pass through their town. In preparation for his arrival, the townspeople would work on the road to make it a smoother path for the king's coming. When necessary, they might even change the path the road followed to make it more direct.

Years ago, President George H. W. Bush came to Houston for a gathering with world leaders. I remember driving along the route that the president would take from the airport to his meeting, and I was surprised to see how clean and beautiful everything was. City officials had cleaned up the graffiti, sidewalks, and streets. They even planted flowers along the roads where President Bush would travel. He was not a king, but we prepared the way for him like people prepared for kings in antiquity. When believers repent, we prepare the way of the Lord.

Isaiah's metaphor is clear: we repent to prepare the way for King Jesus to come into our lives. His choice of language shows that repentance includes lowering ourselves in humility and straightening out our crooked behavior to prepare our hearts to receive our king and his reign of power over our lives.

In week one, we said that when reformer Martin Luther declared that "all of life is repentance," he was saying that repentance is not just a one-time event. Rather, we constantly prepare the way for Jesus, our King, to rule over every aspect of our lives.

We've defined repentance as *changing our minds and reconsidering our strategy for living.* When we repent, we are preparing the way for God's power in our lives.

So how do we prepare the way of the Lord so that we can walk in God's power? Tomorrow we'll dive deeper in to answer that question, but we'll finish today with a review of where we have been.

Week One: Repent and Believe is the operating system for spiritual growth. It's how we rely on God's power in our lives.

Week Two: Obedience works when we change our minds about what we believe first, because belief comes before behavior. We change the way we think to change the way we live.

Week Three: God alone gives us power to change, but we have a part in it too. God's part includes the gift of God's Holy Spirit. Our part focuses on spiritual disciplines that make up our Rule of Life.

Week Four: The Holy Spirit of God indwells followers of Jesus. We do not just live for him. He lives in us and empowers us.

Week Five: Believers repent to be filled with the Holy Spirit. We learn to have faith that God's Spirit is present and working in our lives at all times.

Week Six: Spiritual disciplines are our part in a life of repentance and faith. These spiritual exercises are not done to earn favor with God. Rather, we act in such a way that we can be acted upon by God. We discovered that the primary, internal discipline is to spend time alone with God.

Week Seven: The external discipline of community is essential to relying on God's power. In the community of the church, we know and are known. We are not alone in the journey of following Jesus, and when we devote ourselves to God's community, we experience his power.

Questions for Reflection

What does it look like when believers have a habit of continual repentance?

_____

_____

_____

How does this prepare our lives to receive the reign of King Jesus?

_____

_____

_____

How has this study helped you to change your mind and reconsider your strategy for living?

_____

_____

_____

Prayer

Praise our King who reigns over all the universe but still stooped to enter into his creation, making a way for us to know him. Pray that you would see the beauty of his majesty and treasure him above all – the root of lasting repentance.

SCRIPTURE MEMORY

But you will receive _____ when the
Holy Spirit has come upon you, and
you will be my _____ in Jerusalem and in all Judea and Samaria,
and to the end of the _____. *—Acts 1:8*

NEW IDENTITY
NEW ACTIVITY

Scripture Study

Luke 3:7-14

He [John] said therefore to the crowds that came out to be baptized by him, "You brood of vipers! Who warned you to flee from the wrath to come? ⁸ Bear fruits in keeping with repentance. And do not begin to say to yourselves, 'We have Abraham as our father.' For I tell you, God is able from these stones to raise up children for Abraham. ⁹ Even now the axe is laid to the root of the trees. Every tree therefore that does not bear good fruit is cut down and thrown into the fire."

¹⁰ And the crowds asked him, "What then shall we do?" ¹¹ And he answered them, "Whoever has two tunics is to share with him who has none, and whoever has food is to do likewise." ¹² Tax collectors also came to be baptized and said to him, "Teacher, what shall we do?" ¹³ And he said to them, "Collect no more than you are authorized to do." ¹⁴ Soldiers also asked him, "And we, what shall we do?" And he said to them, "Do not extort money from anyone by threats or by false accusation, and be content with your wages."

Observing the Text

Is John's response to the crowds who desire baptism positive or negative? What does John call them to do in addition to repentance?

_____

_____

_____

What three groups address John directly with the same question? How does he answer each of them?

_____

_____

_____

Interpreting the Text

Describe John's agricultural metaphor in your own words. What do you think is his argument here?

_____

_____

_____

What do John's different responses to the three groups have in common? Why would he give different instructions based on someone's occupation?

_____

_____

_____

Teaching

In Luke 3:7-9, John the Baptist's response to the crowds seeking baptism is surprisingly negative. We may wonder what John knew about their motivation that we don't. However, when we examine the parallel passage in Matthew's Gospel, we see that John's condemnation was directed at Israel's religious leaders, the Pharisees and Sadducees, who had joined the crowd (Matthew 3:7). John knew their hearts and rebuked them because their actions did not match what they professed to believe. They were hypocrites. They claimed Abraham as their father, but they did not behave as the children of Abraham. They did not live as people of faith. That's why John's rebuke included this statement in verses 8-9:

> *Bear fruits in keeping with repentance. And do not begin to say to yourselves, "We have Abraham as our father." For I tell you, God is able from these stones to raise up children for Abraham. Even now the axe is laid to the root of the trees. Every tree therefore that does not bear good fruit is cut down and thrown into the fire.*

In this passage, John uses a metaphor to argue that the kind of fruit that a tree bears reveals the identity of the tree. If there are apples on the tree, we know it's an apple tree. But if we say it's an apple tree, and it bears oranges, then it's not an apple tree after all. And the master of the apple orchard will cut down the tree that does not bear apples. Or as John said it, "Even now the axe is laid to the root of the trees." The same is true of people who profess to be Christians, but whose lives do not bear the fruit of Christ. While they say one thing, they do something else. Their behavior indicates they did not repent and believe in the first place.

John told the Pharisees to "bear fruits in keeping with repentance." If you are from Abraham's family, the family of faith, then you will bear a resemblance to your spiritual father, Abraham. Your identity should determine your activity.

The faithful who listened to this conversation took John's words seriously.

They asked, "What then shall we do?" John's response was very practical.

Have you noticed how some occupations are fraught with common sins? In John's day, tax collectors overcharged people. Soldiers were the police force of the day, and many of them extorted money from the people they were intended to protect. Today, similar occupational sins exist, at least as stereotypes. Salespeople exaggerate the truth. Lawyers twist the truth. Businesspeople pad their expense reports. Laborers slack off when the boss is not watching.

In response to his listeners' question, John said that people who are baptized, or immersed, into a life of repentance and faith have a new identity. They are not defined by their jobs but instead by their relationship to God in Christ. Their new identity then leads to new activities that do not match the common sins in their occupation.

So John said that tax collectors would limit their collections to what people owed. Soldiers would learn to be content with their pay instead of using their power for personal gain. And if anyone had more than he needed, he would share with others who had less.

When followers of Jesus repent and believe, they receive a new identity as the people of God. Our new identity leads to a new activity that looks like the activity of Jesus, showing evidence that our repentance and faith are genuine.

When Jesus gives us a new identity, we don't have to try harder to live a life that looks more like him. Rather, this new way of living becomes more and more natural to us because it is in keeping with our new identity.

Questions for Reflection

How have you seen God's way of living become more natural to you as you grow into your identity as one of God's people? If this doesn't feel true for you, why do you think that might be?

_____

_____

_____

Do the people in your line of work struggle with an occupational sin? What is it? How does your identity in Christ call you to behave differently in your work?

_____

_____

_____

Are you more marked by your culture or occupation than you are led by your identity in Christ? How?

_____

_____

_____

Prayer

Thank God for your identity as a citizen in his kingdom, a child in his family, and a missionary carrying out his purpose. Pray that he would continue to change your patterns of living to fit the identity that he has given you. Praise the Holy Spirit for his matchless power to transform sinners into the image of the Son.

SCRIPTURE MEMORY

But you will _____ when the

_____ has come upon you, and

you will be my witnesses in Jerusa-

lem and in all Judea and Samaria,

and to the _____. *−Acts 1:8*

POWER AND THE SPIRITUAL GROWTH GRID

Scripture Study

Luke 3:15-18

As the people were in expectation, and all were questioning in their hearts concerning John, whether he might be the Christ, ¹⁶ John answered them all, saying, "I baptize you with water, but he who is mightier than I is coming, the strap of whose sandals I am not worthy to untie. He will baptize you with the Holy Spirit and fire. ¹⁷ His winnowing fork is in his hand, to clear his threshing floor and to gather the wheat into his barn, but the chaff he will burn with unquenchable fire." ¹⁸ So with many other exhortations he preached good news to the people.

Observing the Text

What were the people wondering about John?

_____

_____

_____

How does John describe the differences between himself and the one who is coming?

_____

_____

_____

Interpreting the Text

What does the crowd's question about John's identity reveal about their response to him?

_____

_____

_____

What agricultural metaphor does John employ in this passage? What do you think it means?

_____

_____

_____

Teaching

People were ready to make John the Baptist their messiah because they thought so highly of him, but he declared that he was not worthy even to untie the sandals of the true Messiah. Like the Messiah to come, John calls people to repentance, but the Messiah alone would give real power for new life by immersing called people in the Holy Spirit.

There is much debate about what the word "fire" refers to in verse 16. Some say it refers to the kind of power the Holy Spirit gives. Others look at the way Luke uses the word power in other places and consider it a reference to judgment of those who do not repent. Still others believe it refers to a refining fire that God uses to purify his people. While the context gives the most credibility to fire being judgment, we must not get distracted by the use of the word "fire" and miss the main point — repentance and faith are connected to power that only Jesus makes possible. When we repent and believe in Jesus, his work on the cross, and his resurrection from the dead, we are baptized in the Holy Spirit. This baptism is the essential source of power to live the life God makes available to us in Christ.

A life of repentance and faith is a life of relying on God's power.

Your commitment to continually repent and believe functions like an upgraded operating system in your life. As you repent, you will connect with God. As you believe, you embrace your new identity as a citizen in God's kingdom, a child in God's family, and a missionary on God's mission.

Your ongoing repentance and deepening belief grows as you learn to be filled with the Holy Spirit and walk with God by exercising spiritual disciplines. As a disciple of Jesus, you are called to rely on God's power for your life more and more.

But the Christian faith is not a matter of simply following rules. It's about a relationship with God. We learn to live in God's adventure story by listening to his voice in our lives and expressing our faith by obeying him courageously.

God is speaking.

Can you hear him?

Will you obey?

Questions for Reflection

How has this study changed your way of thinking about the Holy Spirit?

_____

_____

_____

What have you learned about the spiritual disciplines that you didn't know before?

_____

_____

_____

How have you grown? What has challenged your previously held beliefs?

_____

_____

_____

Prayer

Praise our Three-in-One God: the Father who calls us, the Son who saves us, and the Spirit who shapes us day after day. Thank him for the way he has made a way for you to know him. Ask him to continue the growth you have experienced over the course of this study.

WEEKLY EXERCISE

POWER AND THE SPIRITUAL
GROWTH GRID

We can connect our repentance and the Spirit's power in our lives directly to the Spiritual Growth Grid. Remember, the activities that God calls us to do are rooted in the identity that he has given us in Christ. Remind yourself of that truth by looking at the Grid below. In our new identity, what do we need power from the Holy Spirit to do?

As you consider the activities that the Holy Spirit empowers, write down your observations about the passages below.

We need the Spirit's power to Listen and Obey. We believe God is the ultimate King who has called us into his kingdom. Through Christ, he made us citizens in his kingdom. As citizens, God has given us his Spirit so that we can listen to and obey what he says.

> *And I will give you a new heart, and a new spirit I will put within you. And I will remove the heart of stone from your flesh and give you a heart of flesh. And I will put my Spirit within you, and cause you to walk in my statutes and be careful to obey my rules.*
>
> Ezekiel 36:26-27

When the Spirit of truth comes, he will guide you into all the truth, for he will not speak on his own authority, but whatever he hears he will speak, and he will declare to you the things that are to come.

John 16:13

Did you suffer so many things in vain—if indeed it was in vain? Does he who supplies the Spirit to you and works miracles among you do so by works of the law, or by hearing with faith— just as Abraham "believed God, and it was counted to him as righteousness"?

Galatians 3:4-6

He who has an ear, let him hear what the Spirit says to the churches.

Revelation 2:7a

Observations:

....

We need the Spirit's power to Love and Serve. We believe God is a Father who adopted us into his family through Jesus' work on the cross. As members of his family, the Holy Spirit empowers us to become the children of God who love and serve.

But to all who did receive him, who believed in his name, he gave the right to become children of God

John 1:12

In this is love, not that we have loved God but that he loved us and sent his Son to be the propitiation for our sins. Beloved, if God so loved us, we also ought to love one another. No one has ever seen God; if we love one another, God abides in us and his love is perfected in us. By this we know that we abide in him and he in us, because he has given us of his Spirit.

1 John 4:10-13

For all who are led by the Spirit of God are sons of God.

Romans 8:14

And because you are sons, God has sent the Spirit of his Son into our hearts, crying, "Abba! Father!"

Galatians 4:6

Observations:

We need the Spirit's power to Go and Multiply. We believe God is a Savior who sent his Son to redeem us. He gives us his Holy Spirit and sends us too, as his missionaries who go and multiply.

> *Jesus said to them again, "Peace be with you. As the Father has sent me, even so I am sending you." And when he had said this, he breathed on them and said to them, "Receive the Holy Spirit."*
>
> John 20:21-22

> *But you will receive power when the Holy Spirit has come upon you, and you will be my witnesses in Jerusalem and in all Judea and Samaria, and to the end of the earth.*
>
> Acts 1:8

Observations:

Get Ready for Group

Write your memorized scripture.

_____

_____

_____

_____

_____

What observations and interpretations of scripture were most meaningful
to you?

_____

_____

_____

_____

_____

Summarize your key takeaway(s) for this week.

_____

_____

_____

_____

_____

What will you tell the group about the results of your exercise this week?

_____

_____

_____

_____

_____

How has this week helped you better understand and apply the Spiritual Growth Grid?

_____

_____

_____

_____

_____

REPENT & BELIEVE

WHO GOD IS	WHAT GOD DID	WHO WE ARE	WHAT WE DO
KING	CALLED	CITIZENS	LISTEN & OBEY
FATHER	ADOPTED	FAMILY	LOVE & SERVE
SAVIOR	SENT	MISSIONARIES	GO & MULTIPLY

Made in the
USA
Monee, IL